...ilations

for Brides

Also by Ellen Sue Stern:

I'm Having a Baby:
Meditations for Expectant Mothers

I'm a Mom:
Meditations for New Mothers

Running on Empty:
Meditations for Indispensable Women

Shortchanged:
*What You Gain When You Choose to
Love Him . . . or Leave Him*

Expecting Change:
The Emotional Journey Through Pregnancy

The Indispensable Woman

I DO:
Meditations
for Brides

·

Ellen Sue Stern

A DELL TRADE PAPERBACK

A DELL TRADE PAPERBACK

Published by
Dell Publishing
a division of
Bantam Doubleday Dell Publishing Group, Inc.
1540 Broadway
New York, New York 10036

The trademark Dell® is registered in the U.S. Patent and Trademark Office.

ISBN: 0-440-50494-5

Printed in the United States of America

Published simultaneously in Canada

July 1993

10 9 8 7 6 5 4 3 2 1

FFG

To Joey, with love.

Best regards,

Ellen L. Stan

ACKNOWLEDGMENTS

I wish to thank the following individuals for your insight and support in the writing of this book:

Jill Lamar: for your wisdom and guidance
Gary Stern: for your generous and wonderful editing
Jill Edelstein: for your love and confidence
My parents, Frank and Rosalie Kiperstin: for your steadfast support
My children, Zoe and Evan: for your patience and understanding.

INTRODUCTION

All our lives women dream of being a bride. Whether it's our first or second marriage, we anticipate with shivers meeting the love of our life, sharing hopes and dreams for the future, walking down the aisle, and joining our lives with our mate forever.

Few experiences in life are more thrilling or meaningful than entering into marriage. There is so much to look forward to. The excitement of being deeply intimate with another human being. The passion and pleasure of exploring our sexuality in a secure, monogamous relationship. The comfort of sharing the little things—reading the newspaper in bed on Sunday mornings—and the big things—choosing our first home, making the decision to have our first baby.

Marriage also involves tremendous emotional challenges. We are asked to face and honestly express our fears and vulnerability, because love cannot flourish unless we are prepared to reveal our real selves. We learn to respect each other's needs for privacy, accept each other's limitations, and continually rekindle our love while coping with the sometimes mundane realities of day-to-day life. We struggle to combine different backgrounds, reconcile unfinished business from our past, and integrate our family of origin with the new family we are becoming a part of.

I Do is a meditative journal to help you celebrate the incredible journey you are beginning, as well as a strategic guidebook for coping with the practical realities of marriage. You and your mate may choose to read all of it together, some of it together, or take turns. Although *I Do* is primarily directed at women, many passages are written to both of you, and are specifically marked with intertwined wedding rings.

Writing this book has taught me a great deal. I have spent the past many months reflecting on the nature of love, what makes for a successful marriage, and what it means to be truly committed to another human being. The end result? In finishing this book I found that I was ready to say those sacred, life-changing words: *I Do*. I hope this book helps both you and me as we walk down the aisle with our hearts full of hope, optimism, and faith.

To have and to hold from this day forward . . .
— *Book of Common Prayer*

Happy New Year! And what a hopeful beginning it is! As you begin the new year, know that you have embarked on one of life's most challenging journeys. You have given your hand and your heart, for better or for worse, in sickness and in health, to love and to honor, till death do you part.

A New Year's Resolution: To make each day worthy of the sacred moment on your wedding day when you turned to your beloved and said the words "I do."

Affirmation: I mean it.

January 2

It is only possible to live happily ever after on a day-to-day basis.
— Margaret Bonano

Our intention is to live happily ever after. But life is no fairy tale, and forever is a long time.

In reality marriage happens day-to-day. Each morning we awaken anew to the pleasures and difficulties of joining lives. Stretching before us are countless opportunities to grow as individuals and as a couple.

Some days go better than others. The success of a marriage is neither cemented nor broken by any single day, rather by weeks and months and years of starting over, each and every day.

Affirmation: Today I begin anew.

It was so cold, I almost got married.
—Shelley Winters

We marry for lots of reasons: Passion. Companionship. Someone with whom to share the present and build the future.

We may also marry to ease our own loneliness. To find solace in the arms of another human being.

It's fine for marriage to provide a safe haven from the endless pressures and storms of life, as long as it isn't the only reason—and especially not the primary reason—for making such a monumental commitment. Ultimately, we each must keep ourselves safe and warm in order to keep the fire burning.

Affirmation: I will kindle my marriage with the fire that burns within me.

BALANCE

> *If I'd known what it would be like*
> *to have it all,*
> *I might have been willing to settle*
> *for less.*

—Lily Tomlin *in* The Search for Signs of Intelligent
Life in the Universe, *by Jane Wagner*

We're tired. Tired of trying to be Jane Pauley, Gloria
Steinem, and Julia Roberts rolled into one.

Marriage needn't pile more pressure on top of the
urgency we already feel to be everything to everyone.
Instead we can—and must—turn to our partner for support. Support for a job well done, an acknowledgment of
how much we do and how much we care, for giving
ourselves a break instead of berating ourselves for falling
short of our own impossibly high expectations.

But don't make him your number-one support system
for slowing down—that has to be YOU! The next time you
feel pressured to do more and be more, look yourself
squarely in the mirror and repeat:

Affirmation: I'm doing enough.

No one worth possessing can be quite possessed.
                    —Sara Teasdale

When we find that special person, we want to hold on for dear life. We fear losing what we waited so long to have.

Yet the harder we clutch, the more pressured and pushed our mate becomes. Like a "caged bird who cannot sing," our beloved is trapped by the intensity of our longing and need.

We must have faith that our partner will choose to be with us out of genuine desire, not because of guilt or obligation. Then love becomes a gift, given with a free and open heart.

Affirmation: Love is a choice.

January 6

> SCENE FROM A MARRIAGE: *The phone rings at your office. It's your husband calling to remind you he's working late, he'll be home around ten. Whoops! He's forgotten that he promised to represent both of you at the church fund-raiser tonight because you're presenting at the special employee-appreciation banquet you've been planning for months. What do you do?*

Anyone can make a mistake. As long as this isn't a pattern, the challenge of the moment is not to get all wound up in anger over his amnesia (real or manufactured) and to find a working solution to the problem instead.

What are your alternatives? Is there someone else who can cover for him at the fund-raiser so that both of you can work? Can he bring his work home and do it later in the evening? Can you leave right after the presentation and relieve him so that he won't have to stay up half the night?

Contemporary work pressures require compromise and goodwill. No one has to be the bad guy. But someone—preferably both of you—needs to bend.

Affirmation: Let's work it out together.

The trouble with some women is that they get all excited about nothing—and then marry him.
                                        —Cher

Cher's caustic warning not to commit in the heat of the moment is well taken. He may be great in bed, but that doesn't mean he'll make a great husband. On the other hand, marital security is no trade-off for sexual passion. Touching and lovemaking are keys to remaining excited —and remaining together.

We mustn't forget what it's like to be in love. The sweetness of hands entwined in a darkened movie theater, the feeling of hearts pounding in an instant of ecstasy, can get buried all too easily beneath the mundane demands of daily life.

Certainly we shouldn't put too much stock in sex. But the bigger trouble is when we marry him and then forget there *is* something to get excited about.

Affirmation: I will make time to make love.

January 8

SCENE FROM A MARRIAGE: Your mother-in-law, whom you usually get along with, makes a sideways comment about how many meals her son is eating out. Feeling defensive, you turn to your husband, counting on him to come through. Instead he makes some lame comment, half agreeing with her, and then changes the subject. How dare he? Isn't he supposed to stick up for you?

Men who would fight to the death for you still tend to cower spinelessly before their mothers.

It's a rotten deal, but instead of castigating him for his betrayal, why not ask nicely for what you want: "If your mother ever criticizes me again, please come to my aid even if you disagree. We can talk about it later, but in that moment I want your support."

This is an example of an ultimatum couched as a request. It's perfectly appropriate, and anyway he needs to learn to stand up to her someday!

Affirmation: "I do" means I promise to support you whenever possible.

Nobody keeps anything to themselves anymore; it's simply not fashionable.

—Cynthia S. Smith

The eighties were an era of self-disclosure: I'll tell you every personal detail of my life and you'll tell me every gritty detail of yours.

We needn't be one hundred percent open books with our mate. We deserve some privacy, and a little mystery, especially about the past.

Besides, some things are better left unsaid. Old love affairs belong in our diaries, not necessarily as part of our dinner conversation with our mate. Revelations of attractions to other people which we have no intention of pursuing are useless fodder for needless jealousy.

Be discriminating. Some things are best confided to a friend.

Affirmation: I'll be discriminating about what I share with my mate.

January 10

Anger repressed can poison a relationship as surely as the cruelest words.

—Dr. Joyce Brothers

We stuff our anger in order to avoid a fight. "What's the point?" we wonder, certain there's no profit in pursuing it. "It won't help," we rationalize, hoping the problems will disappear.

Some do. More often anger sizzles and seethes until we explode. The better strategy is to get it out in the open so that we can get beyond it.

If we don't, anger becomes toxic, poisoning the trust and goodwill necessary for intimacy. Anger is scary, but the sooner we get through it, the sooner we can forgive and go on.

Affirmation: My marriage can survive my anger.

In real love you want the other person's good. In romantic love you want the other person.
—Margaret Anderson

In the first flush of romance we project idealistic expectations on our partner, wanting him to fulfill our every wish and desire.

As love deepens, we come to see our beloved as a separate person. Little by little we stop seeing him as an extension of ourselves and begin to appreciate him for who he really is, perfectly flawed, perfectly human.

As we strip away the illusions, our eyes clear; we are more able to see what's good for *him,* to nurture and know what he needs in order to be whole.

Affirmation: I want what's best for him even if it doesn't always make me happy.

January 12

I know some good marriages—marriages where both people are just trying to get through their days by helping each other and being good to each other.

—Erica Jong

What a surprising definition of marriage from writer Erica Jong, whose characters are more likely to indulge in steamy sexual exploits than sit around sipping tea, being good to each other.

So much for fiction. It may not make for a hot novel, but in my book the best marriage is made up of two individuals each committed to the other's happiness and well-being. Helpmates—lovers who are devoted to serving one another: an old-fashioned idea whose time has come.

Affirmation: We will be good to each other.

Forgiveness is the key to action and freedom.
    —*Hannah Arendt*

It's easy to feel loving when our partner pleases us. The tougher challenge is to accept each other when we fail.

We can wallow in our disappointment, going over and over the details, trapped within the prison walls of our anger and hurt. Or we can forgive. Instead of becoming paralyzed by pain, we must remember we are both fallible. Inevitably we will miss the mark and in so doing wound one another. When that happens, will we respond with anger or with compassion?

Forgiveness frees us to love again. Being able to say, "I understand. It's okay," is the true test of love.

Affirmation: I will find it in my heart to forgive.

LOVEMAKING

January 14

I don't think when I make love.
                    —Brigitte Bardot

Making love can be a comfort and a relief.

We don't have to figure anything out; we get a temporary break from worrying about work piled high on our desk or having to impress anyone with our brilliance.

Sex is one of the few things that improves when we shut off our minds. The less we think and the more we trust our instincts, the better lovers we are.

When our mind *does* interfere, it may be a sign of discomfort. It may be a sign that we should call a momentary halt and speak up, so we can fully relax and enjoy.

Affirmation: My mind is empty, my heart is full.

A journey of a thousand miles must begin with a single step.
—Lao-tzu

No matter how excited we are, it's easy to feel apprehensive at the beginning of a journey. Our stomach churns as we worry about the machinations of making flights, reading maps, getting where we're going in one piece. Going from what's comfortable and heading into the unknown makes even seasoned travelers nervous and uneasy.

Embarking on a marriage can be similarly nerve-wracking. The road looms long and is filled with surprising twists and turns. Only by taking it one single step at a time can we feel secure of our destination.

We will take countless single steps: the first time we hurt our partner and need to swallow our pride and apologize; the first time we're faced with a crisis and need to call on courage we didn't even know we possessed. At each turn, with determination and direction, we put one foot ahead of the other.

Affirmation: Let's go.

DECISION MAKING

January 16

> *SCENE FROM A MARRIAGE: Your sister wants you to go in on an anniversary gift for your parents. She suggests a new TV. Half of a TV is way over your budget, but you're embarrassed to say so. Feeling pushed against the wall, you agree, with the understanding that you'll pay her back over the next six months. Your husband walks in in time to hear the tail end of your conversation. You hang up, look at him sheepishly, and he says, "What in the world did you do that for?!"*

When pressured, we may make decisions over which we feel defensive or regretful. You may be feeling both right now.

Even though you're embarrassed, there are ways to rectify this situation. First, you can explain how pressured you felt and why you made the choice you did.

Second, you need to apologize. Why? For making an executive decision when a vote was called for.

Once you've explained and apologized, you can decide what's best for both of you. Can he live with the contract you've made with your sister? If not, are you willing to retract it, tell her what's affordable, and then give what you can?

Your sister will forgive you if it needs to be a toaster oven instead of a TV. Your husband will forgive you if you reassure him that from now on you'll wait to make important decisions together.

Affirmation: What do you think?

I have always felt that the great high privilege, relief and comfort of friendship was that one had to explain nothing.
—*Katherine Mansfield*

I wish I could say the same for marriage!

To the contrary, we expect our mate to explain his every move, too often assuming the worst rather than giving him the benefit of the doubt.

What a relief it would be to relax with our lover the way we do with a devoted friend. To enjoy the comfort of being understood and accepted without explaining a thing.

Perhaps friendship can be a working model for marriage. Begin by assuming that your mate has your best interest at heart. Try thinking of him as an ally, as your dearest companion in the world.

Affirmation: He's my friend.

INTEGRATION

Ideally, couples need three lives; one for him, one for her, and one for them together.
                                        —Jacqueline Bisset

Merging two lives with distinct personal styles and demanding time schedules poses a challenge to even the most cooperative of couples.

The trick is to respect each person's needs and still make the relationship a priority. This requires clarity—"I need tonight off to be by myself"—and compromise—"Of course I'll go to the hospital with you to visit your great-aunt."

There are times to put ourselves first, other times we need to put our partner first, and still other times when the marriage comes first. Knowing when to do which makes all three possible.

Affirmation: I will be flexible.

In its very essence, love is an appreciation, a recognition of another's value.

— *Robert A. Johnson*

When we value something, we hold it tenderly in our hands. We're careful not to hurt it or drop it or damage it in any way. We spend lots of time looking at it and admiring it, searching for its perfect place upon our shelf.

This is the way we treat someone we love. We recognize this person as a treasure and treat him accordingly.

Affirmation: I will make time to hold you each and every day.

COMMITMENT

January 20

Love is so much better when you're not married.
  —*Maria Callas*

Who wants applesauce when we can bite into a fresh
mango or papaya? As Maria Callas—longtime mistress of
Aristotle Onassis—can testify, exotic fruit may have far
more allure than what sits day after day on our refrigerator shelves.

   Yet, enticing though it may seem, an affair pales against
the deep-running excitement of a committed relationship. Marriage is harder, but infinitely more nourishing.
We opt for a steady, basic diet and savor the subtle sweetness we find.

Affirmation: Commitment is sweet.

A man's home may seem to be his castle on the outside; inside, it is more often his nursery.
—Clare Boothe Luce

My former father-in-law, whom I loved dearly, had one not-so-endearing quality. Although he treated women with great respect, he'd sit at the head of the table, bellowing to his wife of forty years, "Janie, where's the ketchup?" rather than getting up and walking six paces to retrieve it from the refrigerator.

Most of us watched our mothers cater to our fathers; tradition dictated an exchange of dependency. He provided financial support, and she waited on him hand and foot.

Now we have the opportunity to form more equal partnerships. Treating *him* respectfully means we stop coddling him and expect him to act like a responsible adult.

Affirmation: We are both grown-ups.

PROXIMITY

January 22

Sometimes I wonder if men and women suit each other; perhaps they should just live next door and visit now and then.
—*Katharine Hepburn*

Perhaps that worked for Katharine Hepburn, whose three-decade love affair with Spencer Tracy featured adjoining dressing rooms but never the same home address.

I can appreciate how separate domiciles can do wonders for long-term romance. Fights over closet space, toilet-paper rolls, and who used up the hot water have, no doubt, contributed to myriad bleak marital moments.

An occasional visit would probably prevent lots of problems, but oh, think of what we'd miss! Conversations at the kitchen table that last into the wee hours, the unexpected embrace over a mountain of laundry; being right there together when a call comes with good news, or bad.

Those unplanned, unromantic moments can be the most important and magical of all.

Affirmation: I am ready to make a home together.

SCENE FROM A MARRIAGE: *You've been fantasizing about it all day. You even changed the sheets. You put on the new black teddie, light a candle, and curl up, wrapping one leg seductively around his. He yawns, says, "Boy, am I tired," and turns over to go to sleep.*

All right, so usually it's the other way around.

But both women and men take it personally when our partner isn't in the mood. The reason is immaterial.

Whoever initiates it is likely to feel hurt, angry, and disappointed. Hurt that our partner isn't so overcome with passion that fatigue simply disappears. Angry that we've been rejected. Disappointed that our fantasies won't come true.

Saying no calls for sensitivity and compassion. No matter how tired or headachy or disinterested you are, take your partner in your arms and say:

Affirmation: Even if I don't want to make love, I love and want you.

VULNERABILITY

January 24

We have to dare to be ourselves, however frightening or strange that self may prove to be.
                                    —May Sarton

Eventually true intimacy strips us naked. We become incredibly vulnerable before the eyes of our mate.

We only have ourselves, yet that self doesn't always measure up; we don't feel good enough, smart enough, pretty enough. We fear judgment and criticism; how can we know we will still be accepted and loved if we reveal our real selves, flaws and all?

We *don't* know. It takes all the trust in the world and then some to be who we really are. With time and experience we begin to know that we are safe.

Affirmation: I dare to show you who I really am.

SCENE FROM A MARRIAGE: Your oldest friend is in town for the weekend. You've made plans with everyone for dinner out. With spouses. Only yours is being a pill. He doesn't know anyone and he couldn't be less interested. The one time he met Jan, they really didn't hit it off. Besides, there's a great movie on TV. Why should he have to be dragged along when he'd rather stay home?

Because sometimes it's right to do it just because it matters to our spouse. Even if it's inconvenient. Or uncomfortable. Or downright unpleasant.

Part of being married includes going out of our way to accommodate each other. Not every time. But enough of the time that we can depend on coming first when it counts.

This is one of those times. So get dressed, improve your attitude, and decide to enjoy yourself.

Affirmation: It feels good to do something to please the one I love.

FORGIVENESS

January 26

You cannot shake hands with a clenched fist.
—*Indira Gandhi*

Think about the last thing he did that made you mad. As you remember it, close your fist as tightly as you can, digging your fingernails into the palm of your hand.

Now take a deep breath and recall the last thing he did that made you know how much you love him. Slowly open your hand, unwinding each finger like the petal of a rose.

With your open hand, with your best vision of your marriage, reach toward him.

Are you ready to forgive?

Affirmation: Yes.

Never go to bed mad. Stay up and fight.
                    —*Phyllis Diller*

That's the spirit! I'm all for pushing through *if* it gets us somewhere.

There are times when we need to go all ten rounds; other times when we should get out of the ring until we can cool down enough to see things more clearly.

Night fights tend to be especially intense; morning light often brings a better perspective and renewed hope.

Affirmation: I'll fight as long as it makes sense. Then I'll sleep on it.

GLAMOUR

January 28

Glamour is when a man knows a woman is a woman.
　　　　—Gina Lollabrigida

Amen! We want to be treated like the gorgeous sex goddesses we are.

Does that mean we're giving up our hard-earned equality? Is feminism dead?

No! No! No! The more confident we are, the more we value all aspects of ourselves and the more we can celebrate all the ways we are uniquely, wonderfully, glamorously female. And the more we expect the love of our life to appreciate—even worship—our being a woman!

Affirmation: I love being female.

Husbands are like fires. They go out when unattended.
—*Zsa Zsa Gabor*

With nine marriages to her credit, flamboyant Zsa Zsa is an expert on flattering and fawning over men; so much so, I was ready to dismiss her comment as prefeminist foolishness.

Then I thought about it and decided I agree whole-heartedly. Flames of passion do turn to wisps of smoke when left to smolder; the fire dies unless we lovingly tend to our marriage.

But it goes both ways! Husbands need to be tended, and so do wives! Warmth fills our lives if we continue to place kindling on the hearth of our desire.

Affirmation: I'm paying attention.

INDEPENDENCE

January 30

Paradoxically, we cannot navigate clearly within a relationship unless we can live without it.
                    —*Harriet Goldhur Lerner, Ph.D.*

Sometimes we confuse independence with solitary confinement. We think that if we *can* be alone, we'll *end* up alone, when intimacy is what we want so badly.

In fact independence is the best pathway into intimacy. The desperation of loneliness pushes away even the most devoted suitor; having a life of our own and feeling good about it makes us far more appealing and attractive.

We are ready for a healthy relationship when we can stand firmly on our own two feet and walk down that path knowing we'll be fine no matter what adventure lies ahead.

Then we can navigate and negotiate from a position of strength.

Affirmation: If I can live without him, I am ready to live with him.

See everything; overlook a great deal; correct a little.
—*Pope John XXIII*

This may be the best advice I've ever heard for how to conduct oneself in any intimate relationship.

It is especially apt for marriage, where the need for tolerance and understanding is so great. If we can care for each other with open eyes, the willingness to let go of most grievances, and commitment to offer advice or criticism only when it's absolutely necessary—and only from the heart—we will be well on our way to a truly loving union.

Affirmation: I will approach him with a kind and gentle heart.

UNCONDITIONAL LOVE

February 1

If you judge people, you have no time to love them.
— *Mother Teresa*

We yearn for unconditional love, for the blanket acceptance that we are cherished, despite our flaws. Instead we treat our mate as a work in progress, withholding love until he meets our approval. We start out his greatest admirer, then little by little pick him apart. We think marriage gives us the right—and the responsibility—to be his most severe critic.

Judgment is the last thing we need from our mate. Love and judgment are mutually exclusive. Love assumes acceptance; judgment is a form of condemnation.

So what *do* we do with our very real criticism? We either keep it to ourselves or we learn to express it as genuine concern.

Affirmation: I am not his judge.

It is easy to be independent when you've got money. But to be independent when you haven't got a thing—that's the Lord's test.

—Mahalia Jackson

Whether we're staying home, carving out a career, or both; whether we're a two-income family splitting finances down the middle, keeping separate checkbooks, or have signed a premarital agreement with Donald Trump; we are equal partners with an equal say.

A woman I know retired after twenty years as an attorney to stay home and care for her three children. No longer a wage earner, she found herself nervous, defensive, and *asking* her husband for money for ordinary expenses such as groceries. This savvy, successful woman, who weeks before was making a lucrative income, quickly felt—and acted—dependent once she became a stay-at-home mom.

I wanted to shake her. I wanted her to grasp the full value of her contribution. I wanted her to see she was supporting the family—and was entitled to support—every bit as much as before.

Affirmation: Everything we give is of value.

COMBAT

Nobody will ever win the battle of the sexes. There's too much fraternizing with the enemy.
                    —Henry Kissinger

How long can we be combative when our goal is to end up in each other's arms?

This is one of the built-in checks and balances of marriage: Even when a heated conflict erupts, we never completely forget our need for the other person. We aren't willing to stay camped in enemy outposts when we'd rather be fighting on the same side.

Affirmation: He is not the enemy.

Love is the triumph of imagination over intelligence.
—H. L. Mencken

The mega-blizzard on Halloween 1991 left those of us in Minneapolis buried beneath thirty-four inches of snow. With the roads only partly plowed, I set off to surprise Joey, braving shoulder-high snowdrifts with his favorite fried chicken, a bottle of wine, and visions of being snowed in for a week.

Incurable romantic or intrepid lunatic?

Both. I'm glad I went, but I could have waited at *least* until the streets were plowed!

We need to use all our head to make our romance a success, including not taking unnecessary risks. At the same time we must give ourselves over to spontaneous, creative impulses so that passion will thrive, especially in the storms of winter.

Affirmation: Both my head and my heart need to rule.

February 5

If you want to be loved, be lovable.
                                    —Ovid

We can spin our wheels worrying about whether he loves us enough or in the right way or as much as we think we deserve. Or we can use the same energy to work on being our most irresistibly lovable selves.

His love meter is beyond our control. Focusing on what we *can* control pays off in two ways: We get the pleasure of being our best selves and, in concentrating on being a more thoughtful, desirable partner, we attract the kind of love and attention we're looking for.

Affirmation: I am infinitely lovable.

Love means never having to say you're sorry.
—Erich Segal

Actress Ali MacGraw said those now-infamous words to Ryan O'Neal in a tear-jerking scene from the movie *Love Story*. Watching that movie, my first reaction was to heave a great sigh of relief, turn to my then-boyfriend, and retract all my apologies, past and future. I recall thinking, "Easy enough! If I really love someone, I'll never have to say I'm sorry!"

Nothing is farther from the truth. *I'm sorry* are two of the most important words spoken between lovers. The capacity to acknowledge when we've hurt our mate, intentionally or otherwise, to make amends and mean it, goes a long way toward building peace, trust, and intimacy.

Affirmation: Love means often having to say you're sorry.

BEING REALISTIC

February 7

Whenever you want to marry someone, go have lunch with his ex-wife.
> —*Shelley Winters*

Kate used to refer to her husband's ex-wife as "that witch" . . . until she and Jack hit their first rough patch. Suddenly Jack's ex became "a genius."

Wife number one already knew the downside of Jack's foibles and idiosyncrasies. Kate was just beginning to realize that what was charming during the honeymoon had the potential to become downright irritating once they settled back down on earth.

A character reference from his ex-wife or girlfriend isn't really necessary to form a true picture of who he is. When we commit to a partner for life, sooner or later we're going to see all of him—the selfish and the valiant, what makes us cringe and what makes us proud.

Affirmation: My eyes are open.

It is always darkest just before the day dawneth.
        —*Thomas Fuller*

When hopelessness slips over us, it's important to remember the times we've felt this way before—and things worked out for the best.

That doesn't dismiss the pain we feel when we aren't able to connect, when we fall into the muck of seemingly irresolvable differences.

It's okay to feel our despair, even to immerse ourselves in it for a while, as long as we don't allow the darkness to eclipse our hope.

Affirmation: Dawn always comes.

February 9

One thing I know: the only ones among you who are really happy are those who have sought and found out how to serve.
—*Albert Schweitzer*

Loving is infinitely more fulfilling than being loved.

Going out of our way for someone we care about gives us a deep sense of satisfaction. We get back double what we give; the pleasure of serving another person—being there for our beloved just because we want to—is the greatest gift of being in a relationship.

Think about the last time you did something heartfelt for a friend or your mate. Do you remember the look on his or her face? Do you remember how good you felt inside?

Affirmation: The pleasure is mine.

And woman should stand beside man as the comrade of his soul, not the servant of his body.
— *Charlotte Perkins Gilman*

Soul comrades. What a beautiful description of marriage partners at their best—a combination of soul mates and comrades!

Soul mates understand each other intuitively and are devoted to shared spiritual fulfillment. Comrades stand united, working together toward a common goal.

No one on "top," no one on the "bottom," but rather two side by side in perfect equality.

Affirmation: We are soul comrades.

"I KNEW YOU HAD YOUR PERIOD!"

February 11

> *SCENE FROM A MARRIAGE: So you're crabby. So what! He'd be crabby, too, if he had a lousy day at work, came home to a pile of bills, last night's dishes in the sink, and had an awful fight with your mother like you just did. But does he understand? Does he ask you if you want to talk about it? Noooooooo. Instead he says with a smirk, "Is it that time of the month again, honey?"*

Well, maybe it is. And maybe it isn't.

In any case you don't appreciate being patronized or dismissed. Like him there's lots of reasons for how you feel at any given time; unless your menstrual cycle regularly turns you into Sybil, it probably doesn't account for all—or even most—of what's going on inside.

The next time he comes up with this (and remember, he may mean well, even though he's off the mark), tell him that having your period is but a punctuation mark to the rest of your life.

Affirmation: I am a multilayered human being.

Our chief want in life is someone who will make us be what we can.
— *Ralph Waldo Emerson*

One of the best reasons to marry someone is because being with them makes us want to be our very best.

We deserve a partner who inspires us to stretch, to overcome obstacles and develop our most promising gifts.

Being his life partner feels like a "sign." It says, You're an amazing person who's capable of great things. I want to help you do everything in your power to live up to your highest potential.

Affirmation: His love asks the best of me.

MANIPULATION

February 13

I think I can change him. . . . Nobody's ever really loved him before. . . . I'll be the one to do that and then he'll change.

—*Melody Beattie*

We've been conditioned to put endless effort into "fixing" men in order to get their love and affection.

There's a point at which this no longer makes sense: when we invest ourselves at the cost of our own happiness and well-being; when we cross the line between caring and caretaking; when we think we have the power to get him to love himself, which is something only *he* can do, it's time to refocus on our own self-esteem.

Because the fact is there's no such thing as changing him. We can love him. And we can love ourselves enough to accept what he can and can't give without our taking it personally.

Affirmation: Today I will make the commitment to work on myself instead of trying to change him.

I will wear my heart upon my sleeve.
   —from Othello, *by William Shakespeare*

Saint Valentine's Day. A day for romance. A day that takes us back to fifth-grade memories of shoeboxes filled with sticky heart candy and scrawled messages of love.

Many of us wake up today with the same heart-pounding desire that our lover will live up to our most dashing fantasies. Will long-stemmed roses be delivered to the door? Will our hopes be realized? Chocolates? Lace lingerie? At the very least a card scrawled with "I love you."

He, too, may be waiting and hoping. Don't hold back. Don't second-guess him. Today, go all out. Shower him with love and attention. Show all the passion in your heart.

Affirmation: I will love with abandon.

"IT'S YOUR TURN TO DUST AND VACUUM."

February 15

> *SCENE FROM A MARRIAGE: He finally agreed that he'd help you with the housecleaning today—one measly day! Now he's reneging. He says he's got to work out today; if he doesn't get to the club soon, he's going to have a heart attack from all the stress in his life. But what about your life? What about your stress?*

You can beg. You can threaten. You can throw a fit. But ultimately you might as well get real about what's worth a fight and what you can forget.

Choosing your battles—and this may be a worthy one —depends on your bottom line. How important is this issue to your values and integrity? Is it a little thing that bugs you or a potential "relationship breaker"? Would you rather be *right* or work it out?

If taking his turn—after all you clean *every single time*— is truly a matter of partnership, not pride, insist that he fulfill his commitment. But if you're negotiable, say so. No point in grandstanding.

Affirmation: I'm willing to pick my battles carefully.

A master can tell you what he expects of you. A teacher, though, awakens your own expectations.
—Patricia Neal

Marriage can be a loving classroom of adult education in which each partner takes turns being teacher and student.

But we sabotage this delicate process if we believe the object is to satisfy our mate's expectations, both stated and imagined. We stop being adult learners and feel like children, vying to "go to the head of the class." It is up to both of us, in our shifting roles of teacher and student, to create an open atmosphere of mutual safety and respect.

Then we can experience one of the great gifts of marriage, which is the degree to which we rouse each other to dream dreams, to learn and grow and reach for all life holds.

Affirmation: There is no lesson plan.

February 17

It is very easy to forgive others their mistakes; it takes more grit and gumption to forgive them for having witnessed your own.
—Jessamyn West

Why do we fight, apologize, and still feel crummy?

Because long after we've forgiven each other, we're left with the more excruciating struggle of self-forgiveness: for having acted out of fear and insecurity; for angry words we wish we had never said; for having failed to be our best, most loving selves; for making a fool of ourselves in the eyes of our beloved.

The strength of our marriage is tested by times when we blow it. We discover if there's enough trust to reveal our imperfections and still feel deserving of love.

Affirmation: Forgiving him is important. So is forgiving myself.

Earth's crammed with heaven.
> —*Elizabeth Barrett Browning*

When besieged by bills, in-laws, and the inevitable leaky sink, it's easy to miss the transcendent moments of marriage: the glance that says everything; the holy, erotic moment in lovemaking when everything comes together; the amazing moment when you celebrate your first anniversary.

The capacity to delight in these daily glimmers of heaven is vital to balancing the everyday pressures of life on earth.

Affirmation: It's all here for the taking.

EMPOWERMENT

February 19

Some of us are becoming the men we wanted to marry.
                              —*Gloria Steinem*

The good news: We no longer look to men as our ticket to power and achievement.

The not-so-good-news: Some of us have bought the idea that looking *like* men is the ticket to making it in the world.

We needn't compromise our femininity in order to succeed. On the contrary, we can be powerful on our own terms. Both our betrothed and those we face at the bargaining table benefit by the unique sensibility and style women bring. Nurturing, sensitivity, and the ability to negotiate fairly are powerful tools.

Affirmation: I am becoming more myself.

I'm suggesting we call sex something else, and it should include everything from kissing to sitting close together.
—Shere Hite

Recent statistics reveal that on average, American couples make love three times a month.

What I want to know is, Where do they find the time?!

Actually what I want to know is, What about all the other physical touching that's so much a part of expressing love and affection?

When we limit our definition of sex to intercourse and its accompanying foreplay, we skew the real picture of the tenderness and pleasure that passes between marriage partners. The soft brush against the cheek, the playful hug or relaxed shoulder we lay our head on during the ten o'clock news can be as exciting and sensual as the most earthshaking orgasm.

Affirmation: It's all sex. It's all intimacy. It all counts.

RECONCILIATION

February 21

Marriage is the only war in which you sleep with the enemy.
—Anonymous

And thank goodness for that!

When I was first engaged to be married at twenty-two, my Grandma Sophie took me aside and said, "No matter what, make sure and sleep in the same bed. That way if you get in a fight, you nudge him, his arm flops on yours, and pretty soon everything's all right."

It isn't always that simple, of course, but cuddling up goes a long way toward breaking the ice when misunderstanding chills our affections. Sex may not be the remedy of choice, but touching can definitely soften anger and help us inch back from our separate sides.

Affirmation: Move over.

One cannot collect all the beautiful shells on the beach.
　　　—Anne Morrow Lindbergh

Some say monogamy is an unnatural state, that over the course of a lifetime it's human nature to explore attractions to lots of different people.

Diversity gives richness to our experience. So does depth. We can spend our days collecting dozens of shells, all beautiful in their own way, spending a short time turning each one over in our hands. Or we can devote a lifetime to poring over the endless curves and hidden corners of the one, most perfect shell we've chosen to carefully place on our shelf.

Within each shell—within each individual—is the mystery of an entire ocean.

Affirmation: It's all right here.

"YOU COULD STAND TO LOSE TEN POUNDS."

February 23

> *SCENE FROM A MARRIAGE: You're standing in front of the mirror, tugging at the sides of the silk dress you bought especially for the wedding. Your stomach is sticking out. You turn to him and ask, "Do I look fat?"*

This is a simple yes-or-no question.

The right answer is no.

Although men often mistake this question as an earnest query, it's really insecurity speaking solely in search of reassurance.

If you're worried this means you don't have an "honest marriage," don't be. She knows exactly how she looks; she's her own worst critic.

Trust me on this one: What she wants from you is compliments, even if it means stretching the truth.

Affirmation: You look great!

It all starts with self-esteem. Then you can know and empathize more profoundly with someone else.
—Shirley MacLaine

When we're feeling shaky, we quickly run out of "spare change." No matter how much love we feel, we experience our partner's pain as pressure; his simplest need translates into an impossible imposition.

In contrast, when we feel confident, we are able to tune in to our mate's feelings and needs without it costing us. We can afford to see him as separate from ourselves. We can put ourselves aside and concentrate on loving him, which in turn makes us feel better about ourselves.

Affirmation: Loving him starts with loving myself.

February 25

It takes a lot of courage to show your dreams to someone else.
—*Erma Bombeck*

He's hurt because you talked on the phone while flipping through his pictures from Jamaica. You're hurt because he looked away when you read him that passage from your journal.

It *is* scary to share what's really important to us. We want to be known truly, known for who we are. We want to unwrap our heart from within its silvery tissue paper, a little at a time.

We do so with trepidation that our dreams will be ridiculed or dismissed. And we do so with hope that we will finally be understood—seen—and loved.

Affirmation: My dreams are fragile. Handle with care.

The pessimist looks at opportunities and sees difficulties; the optimist looks at difficulties and sees opportunities.
—*Anonymous*

On our wedding day we raise the ritual glass, toasting a full and rich life together.

But there are times ahead when the glass appears half empty. Then we need to look more closely at what we have, as well as what's missing.

What's missing is a mirage; the empty space in the glass is an opening, an opportunity to fill our lives with greater hope.

Affirmation: My cup is half full.

February 27

It is ridiculous to think you can spend your entire life with just one person. Three is about the right number.
— Clare Boothe Luce

As we travel through life with another person, we are constantly in the process of changing. No one stays the same. The commitment to joining lives doesn't give us license to become static or stale, but rather the opportunity to keep growing.

Is the twenty-year-old girl who becomes the thirty-five-year-old woman who ripens into the seventy-five-year-old matriarch just one person? Or does the person we marry, although familiar, have the potential to be fresh and new with each passing day?

Marriage—and life—is a dynamic process. Each person changes and surprises us through their ongoing journey of personal growth.

Affirmation: We are both growing.

You are never fighting for the reason you think you are.
—Barbara De Angelis

She's furious at him for coming home twenty minutes late from work. (If he really cared about her, he'd be on time!)

He's had it with her piles of clothes all over the bedroom. (Isn't there room for *him* in their home?)

She's pissed that he told their best friends they'd go skiing this weekend. (How come he makes all the decisions? Besides, she's a lousy skier!)

The issue at hand is often a smoke screen for what's smoldering underneath. We can only get through our problems if we're willing to get down to what's really going on.

Affirmation: The sooner we get real, the sooner we'll work it out.

SELF-CARE

February 29

To love oneself is the beginning of a lifelong romance.
—Oscar Wilde

Today on Leap Year, do something to express your love to *yourself.*

Sometimes in loving our mate we lose track of the need to focus on our own self-care. When we go out of our way to pay attention to ourselves—a long-awaited shopping trip or a bubble bath by candlelight—we end up refreshed, replenished, and more able to give.

Think of today as an extra twenty-four hours—a gift of sorts—in which you renew your romance with someone you love—*you.*

Affirmation: Today is my day to love myself.

Generally, by the time you are Real, most of your hair has been loved off, and your eyes drop out and you get loose in the joints and very shabby. But those things don't matter at all, because once you are Real you can't be ugly, except to people who don't understand.

—from "The Velveteen Rabbit," by Margery Williams

At first we are entranced by our mates. Their eyes shine, their hair glows, their conversation fascinates, their wardrobe beguiles.

As we become more familiar with each other, we see more of what is real. Sometimes our eyes are shiny, other times they're glazed with fatigue. Some days our hair looks like we stepped right out of a Clairol ad; other days we can't do anything with it. Sometimes we're stimulated by each other; sometimes we're bored. And sooner or later we've worn everything in our closet!

We trade the newness for comfort. For the deep, sustaining pleasure of not having to put on a show, secure in knowing that we are loved and accepted for who we *really* are.

Affirmation: I'd rather see the real you.

FIGHTING

The time to win a fight is before it starts.
—*Frederick W. Lewis*

Fights are one way spouses compete for power. We use the relationship as an arena in which to assert supremacy.

One side may "win," but both parties are bruised in the process. In most heated arguments between mates the "victor" stands alone in the corner, while the vanquished storms off, defeated and demoralized.

If there's really something to fight about, get it out in the open with the intention of *working it out* rather than winning. Then both sides can go at it fearlessly, knowing that:

Affirmation: This relationship is worth fighting for.

*SCENE FROM A MARRIAGE: Okay, so you didn't
expect him to show up with anything, even though you found
him the perfect hat just like the one he admired in the catalog.
He surprises you! You excitedly tear open the tissue paper
. . . new potholders. You could kill him! You don't know
what to say.*

Say thank you.

No matter how disappointed you are, no matter how
convinced you are—at this moment—that not only does
he not love or understand you, he never will—say thank
you.

Thank you for remembering our anniversary. Thank
you for trying. Thank you for making the effort.

Now on to next year: Make a date to shop together for
your anniversary gifts. Settle on a price range and make it
a romantic outing where each of you chooses what you
really want.

Affirmation: Effort counts.

SEPARATENESS

March 4

> *I am missing you*
> *far better than I*
> *ever loved you.*
> —*Harold Bloomfield*

Sometimes it feels great to stomp off in the middle of an argument. We blow off steam, complain about him to anyone who'll listen, and nurse our fantasies of leaving him so that he'll come to his senses and give us the adoration we deserve.

In the process we come to *our* senses. We start appreciating—and adoring—him! When we give ourselves permission to run away, we feel more free to return to him. When we let ourselves miss him, we realize, once again, how much we love him.

Affirmation: I will love you when I'm with you.

If you don't like someone, the way he holds his spoon will make you furious; if you do like him, he can turn his plate over into your lap and you won't mind.
—Irving Becker

When we're in love, even his most annoying traits are endearing; his possessiveness seems sexy, his money fears fiscally responsible. We overlook it when he forgets our birthday and call him a curmudgeon when he grumbles about Thanksgiving at our parents'.

But when we're not getting along so well, the very same qualities are subject to harsher interpretation. Now his jealousy seems immature, his money tightness a bore. His unwillingness to accommodate us means he doesn't really care, and we want to call him all sorts of unseemly names.

Has he had a complete personality change? Probably not. Is the magic gone? Hopefully not, unless the flame has really died—which isn't likely. Don't worry. Soon enough you'll find the charm in him again.

Affirmation: He's the same person I fell in love with.

March 6

> *THE NEW MAN*
> *I worry sometimes*
> *maybe Bob has gotten too much in touch with*
> *his feminine side. Last night*
> *I'm pretty sure he faked an orgasm.*
> —*Lily Tomlin in* The Search for Signs of Intelligent
> Life in the Universe, *by Jane Wagner*

Okay, let's be honest.

It's great that he can talk about his feelings, but once in a while we'd like him to shut up and throw us on the bed.

We want a sensitive, nineties-style guy with a little Cave Man thrown in for good measure. We want a man who is independent *and* approachable, powerful *and* gentle, in touch with his feminine side as well as his masculine core.

If we can be both soft and strong, we won't have to fake a thing.

Affirmation: Women and men are both evolving.

Women need to stop catering their relationships and start being at the party.

—*Ellen Sue Stern*

I wanted to do something nice for Joey, so I threw him a forty-first birthday party. He took the day off so that we could spend it in a leisurely manner; I spent all day running around like a nervous wreck buying flowers, picking up the cake, and picking up my house so that it would look perfect when the guests arrived.

I missed the point. The best birthday gift would have been my undivided attention. We both would have had a better time.

Affirmation: It's my party too.

PARTNERSHIP

March 8

And it is still true, that no matter how old you are—when you go out in the world, it is best to hold hands and stick together.
—*Robert Fulghum*

When we were little, the buddy system made lots of sense: a dependable partner with whom to clasp hands and stick close as we tested the water.

The buddy system still makes sense. Each morning we awaken and venture out into the world with the confidence that we are securely in each other's minds and hearts. Knowing our destinies are linked. Knowing we can count on our beloved to look out for us—no matter where we are—and that we will come back together and curl up, once again, in the safety of each other's arms.

Affirmation: Take my hand.

Without inner peace, it is impossible to have world peace.
—Fourteenth Dalai Lama

And without inner peace, it is impossible to sustain a peaceful, nurturing marriage.

Too often our love relationship is marked by strife, where we feel pressured and embattled instead of accepted and supported in our spiritual journey.

Whether we seek it through prayer, meditation, or fellowship, each of us is responsible for cultivating our own inner peace. Then our marriage can be a safe haven. Then we can lend our hands in building a better, more peaceful world.

Affirmation: My marriage is a place of peace.

March 10

Although we adjust and adapt and compromise and make do, we sometimes may hate the married state for domesticating our dreams of romantic love.
                                        —Judith Viorst

Domesticity doesn't have to mean we settle for a boring and tedious routine. On the contrary, making a home together is one of life's most exciting, romantic adventures.

The key word is *we*. *We* hang curtains and negotiate closet space. *We* sit down together and dig into the perfect omelet *he* has surprised me by whipping up.

Meanwhile love grows like houseplants, quietly in the corner, with the constants of light, water, and time.

Affirmation: Doing dishes together can be romantic.

Q. Why did the man cross the road?
A. Who knows? Why do men do anything?

Male bashing—though endlessly entertaining—is ultimately counterproductive.

We patronize men, then wonder why they're reluctant to put themselves on the line. When we assume that men just don't get it, that women are inherently superior, we seriously limit what's possible between us and our mate. We accentuate our differences and are both diminished in the process.

There's probably a good reason for why he crossed the road. Ask. And listen.

Affirmation: I want to know.

FEMALE BASHING

Take my wife. . . . Please!
    —*Henny Youngman*

Jokes that make fun of women are equally disrespectful.

Whether the target is mothers-in-law, Jewish princesses, or blondes (the newest craze), putting down women is seen as everything from retrograde "male bonding" to an insidious source of violence against women. It's cheap, and there's nothing funny about it.

Better to cut the jokes and take the time to understand each other . . . and love each other. . . . Please!

Affirmation: No more jokes.

Dear God. Dear stars, dear trees, dear sky, dear peoples. Dear Everything. Dear God.
　　　—from The Color Purple, *by Alice Walker*

Let us begin each day of our marriage giving thanks from the bottom of our hearts for the chance to love and to be loved.

Before we met our mate, we may have yearned for someone with whom we could feel safe and understood, someone who made us wake up every morning looking forward to another day.

Now that we've found each other, let's never take what we have for granted. Let's count our blessings, saying thank you to the stars, the trees, the "everything" for the love we're so fortunate to have in our lives.

Affirmation: Thank you.

IDENTITY

Being married gives one position like nothing else can.
—Queen Victoria

How's that for an anachronism?

Maybe in Queen Victoria's day, a wedding ring bestowed automatic status and respectability. Not so anymore.

For most contemporary women an M.R.S. degree is no longer, symbolically or otherwise, an honorable pursuit. Rather we marry when we meet a man whom we love and respect, who is our equal, with whom we can pursue a full and meaningful life. We may enjoy the cultural perks of partnership, but our identity doesn't rest on being his wife any more than his comes from being our husband.

Each of us is in a position to make our own name in the world.

Affirmation: I'm still me.

If married couples did not live together, happy marriages would be more frequent.

—Friedrich Nietzsche

Maybe so. But then again, the challenge of marriage is to live together *and* be happy. Or, as the famous Stephen Stills song goes, to "love the one you're with"—even on days when we feel like running away, even when we wonder why we ever left our last lover or fantasize about how much better life could be with someone else.

But that someone else would be just as hard to love if we woke up with him every morning. Loving a phantom or fantasy is easy. Loving the real person sitting across from us at the breakfast table takes true commitment and imagination.

Affirmation: I want to be here.

SEX

In my sex fantasy, nobody ever loves my mind.
—Nora Ephron

Our minds need a rest. We yearn for a reprieve from the constant mental pressure of making lists, making deals, and making sense. In the comfort and safety of marriage we can let down and let loose our most erotic and secret selves.

It's fun to be a sex object, to indulge in our wildest fantasies and give ourselves over to the pleasures of the flesh.

This is one of the perks of marriage: to turn off our minds occasionally, tune in to other parts of ourselves, and turn on.

Affirmation: He loves my body too.

"How to Be His Last Wife."
      —Cosmopolitan *cover story, 1971*

Believe it or not, this seemingly serious article appeared in *Cosmo* when I was sixteen years old. Back then it was considered a subject of grave and strategic importance!

Perhaps it still is. Sexist language aside, I know plenty of couples interested in essentially the same goal: how to do everything in their power to be each other's mate for life.

In this day and age of peak divorce rates, women can't take for granted being his "last wife" any more than men can blithely assume they will be her "last husband." It works both ways. And it doesn't work unless we give it everything we've got.

Affirmation: I trust our love will last.

March 18

Love is the one power that awakens the ego to the existence of something outside itself.
—_Robert A. Johnson_

We are all profoundly nearsighted, only able to perceive the world as it revolves around us.

Love expands our vision. We are able to see past our limited vantage point and appreciate another human being's perspective. With vision comes clarity. As we see more clearly, empathy develops. We begin to truly understand each other—who each of us is, what we're made of, and what we need in order to be fulfilled.

Affirmation: I see you.

Look hard at yourself. Look hard at how you feel, really, about the people among whom fate so indifferently dropped you.
—*Alice Walker*

There are billions of people in the world, so why him?

Whether he was a stranger sharing a taxi or the boy next door, whom we meet, fall in love with, and marry is in large part serendipity. Seemingly chance encounters forever alter our lives.

There's something about fateful meetings. It's like a whisper in the background that says, "This is the one. We are meant for each other."

And so we are; as lovers, as guides, as teachers; to heal the past, treasure the present, and create the future.

Affirmation: I'm so grateful we found each other.

INDIVIDUALITY

Every being cries out to be read differently.
—Simone Weil

What sweeter bliss than to be thoroughly understood?

Although marriage draws us closer and closer together, we remain separate human beings, each with a fundamental need to be seen—heard—known for who we really are.

But sometimes our drive for union supersedes the need to express our individuality. We rob our marriage when we dilute our uniqueness, hiding parts of ourselves or seeking common ground at the expense of authenticity.

Our individuality—not our sameness—is our best gift to each other.

Affirmation: I will try to understand you.

Life is but an endless series of experiments.
—Mohandas K. Gandhi

When we focus on "end goals" of marriage—security, companionship, someone with whom to grow old—we miss out on the journey.

It's like taking a car trip halfway across the country and spending the whole time staring at the speedometer and worrying about when we'll arrive. Half the fun is savoring the scenery, experimenting with new routes, and spontaneously stopping at out-of-the-way rest stops. What's least planned often turns out to be most unforgettable.

This is how we should travel through marriage: with a flexible itinerary and a spirit of adventure.

Affirmation: Let's go.

March 22

If we are unhappy without a relationship, we'll probably be unhappy with one as well.
—Melody Beattie

Everything we are we bring with us into our marriage. Our sadness or stresses don't automatically disappear because we now have someone with whom to share them.

Marriage illuminates both the good and the bad. Our achievements shine more brightly through the reflection of our partner's eyes, but problem areas become more glaring as well. If anything, being in a relationship makes it that much more pressing to confront issues that keep us from being happy and whole. Because no matter how loved we are, it's still just us alone looking in the mirror.

Affirmation: My marriage can help me heal, but being happy is up to me.

"HOW CAN I BE OVERDRAWN WHEN I STILL HAVE CHECKS?"

March 23

SCENE FROM A MARRIAGE: The mail comes. An overdraft notice. Damn it! You blew it again! Maybe you should hide it. Maybe they'll put it back through. Maybe you should start carrying cash!

Or maybe you should think about having him take over —or at least participate in keeping track of money and paying the bills.

We have different talents. We can—and should—try to improve; bouncing checks is costly and naturally frustrates your mate. One way to improve is by asking him to tutor you in money management. You'll learn something, and he'll feel less out of control.

Then again, some people just can't add two and two, in which case both of you need to accept your limitations. If he's great with money, let him handle it. If you're terrific at housepainting, let him off the ladder. Make the most of what each of you has to give.

Affirmation: Job-sharing means that each of us takes different jobs.

SELF-FORGIVENESS

March 24

Even God cannot change the past.
                    —*Agathon*

We make mistakes, say terrible things, and wish to God we could turn back time and start over.

We can't go backward any more than the sun can set in the east. Preoccupation with regret ties our stomach in knots and stymies our capacity to move forward.

What's done is done. What lies ahead is the opportunity to ask forgiveness and do a better job next time.

That's all we can ask of ourselves. It is more than enough.

Affirmation: I can change the future.

A simple enough pleasure, surely, to have breakfast alone with one's husband, but how seldom married people in the midst of life achieve it?

—Anne Morrow Lindbergh

The first time we went on a vacation, I remember being amazed by the quiet—and the closeness—we experienced. Time for just the two of us, on break from job pressure and the incessant jangling of the telephone, immediately renewed romance and intimacy.

We forget what it's like to share in a leisurely manner, quality time—talking or not talking, eating bagels and reading the Sunday paper, simply enjoying the pleasure of each other's company.

Make it a priority to break bread together at least once a week—no phone, no work, no in-laws. Do whatever it takes to make it happen.

Affirmation: This marriage is important enough to find time alone.

FEAR

March 26

*There were two reasons I didn't want to marry Mark: first of all,
I didn't trust him. And second of all, I'd already been married.*
—Nora Ephron

The first should have been reason enough, especially for
Nora Ephron's character in *Heartburn,* whose husband is
having an affair while each day her pregnant body grows.
But the second reason is a trickier reality for many of us
who have experienced the pain of divorce.

If, for either or both of you, this is a second marriage,
it's wise to be aware of the understandable fear and mis-
trust you bring with you. It may not be fair, but the past
inevitably affects the present; if you've been hurt or disappointed before, it may take time to trust again.

Use your experience and insight as a guide. As you feel
safe, you can risk more and more.

Affirmation: That was then. This is now.

It's possible you will never "love back" to the degree and quantity that people love you. You may have to relax about settling up your emotional accounts.
　　　　　　—Mary Kay Blakely

Believe it our not, married couples are competitive about love—not how much they get but how much they give.

"I love you," he says. "I love you more," she counters, upping the ante. He pulls out the time he waited an hour and a half to drive her home in a snowstorm; she plays her trump card—the sweater it took six months to knit.

The truth is we love differently. And we worry that somehow it isn't enough. But it is. We give in the ways we know how, using whatever emotional currency we have in our bank.

Affirmation: I am in the black.

SELF-CONSCIOUSNESS

March 28

The impulse to save something good for a better place later is the signal to spend it now.
—Annie Dillard

I just read an interview with an editor at *Mademoiselle* magazine who, talking about "dating don'ts," said, "Men are turned off by women who say too much about themselves on the first date."

God! I thought. Hasn't anything changed?! Her words evoked memories of being sixteen years old, trying to act subdued so that boyfriends wouldn't feel overwhelmed by my personality. Trying to space anecdotes so that I wouldn't totally monopolize the conversation.

Maybe that's what it still takes to get dates, but it's a lousy idea for marriage. I say pull out the stops.

Affirmation: What am I saving it for?

I think it's worth noting that I was once at a party at which a man said quite loudly, "You look fine without makeup," and eight women turned around, each thinking it was their husband.
— Anna Quindlen

Almost all of them say it, and *none* of us believe it.

We don't have to. If wearing lipstick and eyeshadow makes us feel prettier, sexier, more confident, then by all means we should wear it and enjoy it.

Of course it's a bonus if he really finds us just as attractive "au natural." It's also nice when he notices our efforts at special effects. It's fun to occasionally flaunt a more dramatic look and receive some serious looking in return.

Fact is, it really doesn't matter. Because makeup is one thing women do for themselves.

Affirmation: I like how I look.

THE HIGH SCHOOL REUNION

March 30

> *SCENE FROM A MARRIAGE: It's been ten years and you're all a flutter. Will anyone recognize you? Will they notice you've lost twenty pounds? Hey, there's your prom date from senior year. Gee, he's balding, but he still has those eyes. Your husband looks as if he's about to die of boredom. Should you have come alone?*

Sometimes it's best to go solo instead of letting him cramp your style or make you self-conscious. Why should you have to take care of *him* when by all rights you should be enjoying yourself?

There are times to integrate each other into separate parts of your lives and times you should kiss each other good-bye, just for the evening, and each go your own way. And remember, you can always take along your most flattering picture of him.

Affirmation: We are strong enough to go our separate ways.

I'm trying to get him to love himself so that he'll love me.
—*Anonymous*

We're willing to be his mother, his therapist, his maid. We knock ourselves out encouraging him, reforming him, and cheering him on so that he'll get it together and finally give *us* the love we need!

This is a bad investment.

Number one, no amount of effort on our part can make him love himself—that's up to *him*. We'll just get exhausted and resentful.

Number two, it's better to concentrate the same energy on loving *ourselves*. This is a better bet all around. We automatically benefit from the effort, we're more able to love and appreciate him, *and* he might learn by our example.

Affirmation: I can show him how lovable he is, but I can't make him love himself.

LAUGHTER

April 1

A difference of taste in jokes is a great strain on the affections.
—Anonymous

The husband of one of my friends called her at work to say that urgent business had come up, making it impossible for them to go on the trip to Mexico for which she'd just bought the tickets.

He played it straight despite her panic, then anger, and finally shouted, "April Fool!" just before she burst into tears.

She was so relieved, she wasn't sure whether to thank him or hang up on him.

Jokes can be great as long as they don't get out of hand. Laughing together can be as intimate as the most tender lovemaking; it pulls us together and makes life more palatable.

As long as it's only once a year.

Affirmation: I'm willing to lighten up.

Life is messy.
        —Zoe Stern

When we get stressed out, we tend to take it out on the person closest to us—our mate.

We whine or dump or blame him for what's difficult in our lives. When the blender breaks or the car stalls inconveniently, we snap at him for the mess we're in. After all, *somebody must be to blame!*

Of course no one's to blame. As the popular saying goes, "Stuff happens," and when it does, we're better off joining forces and finding solutions.

Affirmation: Let's help each other clean up.

SEX

April 3

Men complain that women demand reassurance or expressions of love. The Japanese recognized this need . . . after a night of lovemaking, the man had to produce a poem and have it delivered to his love before she awakened.
—Anaïs Nin

We make mad, passionate love and then he rolls over with a sigh of contentment and falls asleep.

Meanwhile we lay awake, having conversations in our head, wishing he'd say something—anything—to confirm the communion of mere seconds before.

A few words—"I love you." A simple gesture—a hug or simple touch on the forehead.

It needn't be poetry. As long as it's sweet.

Affirmation: Afterplay is as important as foreplay.

I hated my marriage, but I always had a great place to park.
—Woody Allen

There are days when our marriage seems more a convenience than a joy, when we treat our spouse like a parking attendant instead of the passionate love of our lives.

That's okay. A good match needs a little bit of the magical *and* the mundane. As anyone who has circled a parking lot for the perfect spot knows, finding it requires both.

Affirmation: Some days are more magical than others.

"THE LASAGNA IS GETTING STIFF."

April 5

SCENE FROM A MARRIAGE: He's late. Again. He promised he'd be home by 6:30, and now it's 7:05. The table's set, and the lasagna you made from scratch is losing its magic by the moment. You know he has a deadline. You know it's rush hour. You should give him a break. But you don't really feel like it.

Of course not.

You're angry, and you should be. He said he'd be there, and if he can't make it, the least he can do is let you know.

Meanwhile go ahead and start. Put his in the oven and sit down and eat. It may not be the lovely dinner you imagined but it's better than the evening—and the food —being ruined.

When he gets home, let him eat *before* you tell him you're angry. This time you'd appreciate an apology. Next time you'd appreciate a call.

Affirmation: It's my responsibility to ask for what I want.

Most women would rather have someone whisper their name at optimum moments than rocket with contractions to the moon.
—Merle Shain

Yes! Yes! Yes!

Orgasms are exciting, while they last. But nothing is more exciting than being cradled in our lover's arms and hearing our name tenderly whispered long after we've landed back on earth.

This is the sweetest intimacy of all—in the moment of ecstasy and surrender, to feel secure, beyond the shadow of a doubt, that we are known, recognized, and loved.

I bet that's what men want too.

Affirmation: Say my name. Softly. Again.

April 7

One half of the world cannot understand the pleasures of the other.

—*Jane Austen*

An old-fashioned woman writer with a viewpoint that will never go out of style.

A hundred years later women of the 1990s express the same sentiment: Men and women are worlds apart in our pleasures and tastes.

We tend to give what we'd like to get instead of giving what really matters to our mate. Taking the time to understand each other's wants and needs, especially when it's something that we couldn't care less about, is one of the ways we say, "I love you and I'm paying attention to what makes you feel good."

Celebrating his birthday with pizza in front of a TV during the football game instead of over a romantic candlelit dinner for two may not seem like much of a party. But, then, it isn't your birthday. Yet.

Affirmation: Our differences are worth celebrating.

And God blessed them, and God said unto them, be fruitful and multiply.

—Genesis 1:27, 28

There are many ways to be fruitful in marriage.

If parenthood is part of your creative vision, and you are fortunate enough to have a child together, know that it will be one of your most fruitful endeavors.

If, however, you remain childless—whether by choice or by chance—your marriage will be every bit as much a blessing.

Affirmation: Creativity takes many forms.

DISCRETION

April 9

The genius of communication is the ability to be both totally honest and totally kind at the same time.
— *John Powell*

Sometimes we blunder in our attempt to be perfectly candid. We say too much. We blurt out the "truth" when a little discretion is in order.

The truth is, there are lots of ways of seeing things and lots of ways of saying things.

Brutal honesty rarely serves our partner; often it's a cheap shot or a cover for criticism.

If there's something you need to say to your loved one, remember to say it lovingly, as if holding his heart in your hands.

Affirmation: I will choose my words carefully.

*The American marriage ideal is one of the most conspicuous
examples of hitching our wagon to a star.*
            —*Margaret Mead*

Which may be why so many marriages run out of steam.

We start out at a fast clip, our hopes and dreams sometimes racing ahead of what's possible. When we're
brought back down to earth, we feel disillusioned; we're
forced to slow down and reevaluate our expectations.

It's important to stay grounded. But it's also important
to aim high.

**Affirmation: I'm keeping one foot on the ground
and one eye on the stars.**

INTENTION

April 11

Love is an act of will—namely, both an intention and an action.
—*M. Scott Peck*

We wait to feel love's inspiration before acting lovingly toward one another.

But real love has little to do with the lightning flash we experience in the flushes of romance. Intention is what separates infatuation and intimacy—the abiding commitment to stand by our beloved with tangible action, going out of our way even if we're not feeling particularly passionate or inspired. Making the effort and letting the ecstasy follow.

True acts of love are absolutely intentional: We make a powerful choice to act on our conviction and commitment.

Affirmation: I will think of three concrete ways I can show my love for you, and then I will do them.

"Spiritual surrender" is intentional. It is the result of the free and unencumbered use of one's will.
—Gerald G. May

The need to surrender is one of the great paradoxes of love.

Surrender may seem like giving up. Or giving in. But in reality we are strengthened when we actively choose to make ourselves vulnerable. We are empowered by sharing our deepest self with another person, offering him or her our heart, our soul, our life.

Surrender is an act of free will. A sacred trust.

Affirmation: I freely give myself over to you.

April 13

SCENE FROM A MARRIAGE: You're late for therapy. He looks perfectly nonchalant, refusing to weave through rush-hour traffic in order to make a little time. "C'mon!" you want to scream at him. Instead you drum on the dashboard, wishing you had married someone a little more aggressive. It's a tough world out there, right?

Right. And we make it even tougher when we transfer our anxiety to our mates, wishing they'd do something to make us feel better.

He may not maneuver like a New York cabbie, but that doesn't entitle you to act like a hysterical passenger.

If you make it to your appointment, you might consider bringing up how you felt in the car. Perhaps you can strategize ways to deal with your panic, such as starting out earlier, getting a car phone, or being the designated driver.

Or you might learn to meditate. Sit back in the front seat, close your eyes, and breathe. Then tell yourself:

Affirmation: We'll get there when we get there.

Perfect love, I suppose, means that a married man and woman never contradict one another, and that both of them always feel the same thing at the same moment, and kiss one another on the strength of it.

—*D. H. Lawrence*

"What blarney!" as D. H. Lawrence goes on to say.

There is nothing perfect about couples who never disagree with each other. (Ever been around one? It's *spooky*!) And there is nothing perfect about couples who only feel close when they are are in total sync. (Is this a couple or a cult?)

What's more perfect is the freedom to be ourselves with our mate; what's more perfect is the kiss that's inspired by an appreciation of our differences.

Affirmation: We are perfectly different.

EFFORT

April 15

Nothing on Earth is more gladdening than knowing we must roll up our sleeves and move back the boundaries of the humanly possible once more.

—*Annie Dillard*

Marriage is tough, physical labor.

With glad hearts we roll up our sleeves and prepare to tackle the challenges ahead. We move mountains to transcend barriers that keep us from loving one another. We work up a sweat pushing ourselves beyond where we have been before, welcoming the opportunity to stretch and grow.

No wonder we feel achy. No wonder we feel exhilarated.

Affirmation: We have our work cut out for us.

Other people do not have to change for us to experience peace of mind.

—Gerald G. Jampolsy, M.D.

We fall into the trap of thinking that our happiness depends on our mate. If he's in a good mood, we feel lighter, freer to pursue our own pleasure. If he's crabby, we feel compelled to fix him so that he won't cramp our style or ruin our day.

This is a waste of time. Compassionate detachment is a better way to go. Then we can refocus on our own capacity to create peace and joy. The moral is: Love him, but leave him alone when you need to.

Affirmation: My peace of mind is purely up to me.

SURRENDER

April 17

Let your heart be wholly empty; then only will it be filled.
                                        —*Krishnamurti*

Making room for love—whether by emptying our heart
of resentment and desire or emptying our schedule to
make time for our beloved—is essential if we are to have a
fulfilling relationship.

   This may mean releasing old anger that's getting in the
way. Or putting the answering machine on to eliminate
unnecessary distractions.

   Both require a willingness to let go and let love in.

Affirmation: My heart is ready to be filled up.

I don't care how you feel. I only care how I feel!
                    —Evan Stern

Only a child could so unabashadly blurt out what is often true for so many of us, though we're loathe to admit it.

It's not that we don't care about his feelings. It's just that we care more about our own!

When we are firmly in our "adult mode," we can be loving and empathetic; we can put our partner's needs ahead of our own. Other times we are driven by the small child within us, desperate to be acknowledged, demanding to come first!

This doesn't make us selfish, just human.

Affirmation: Sometimes I feel like a child.

DOUBTS

April 19

The "I do" that took approximately ten minutes to pronounce will be followed by ten incredulous years of asking, "I did?"
—*Mary Kay Blakely*

It's easy to say "I do." It's harder to continually renew our vows in light of the complex accommodation required to live day in and day out with another person.

Some days we may be absolutely sure of our decision. We'd do it again in an instant! Other days we may question whether we made the right decision. That's okay. It's perfectly natural to constantly reevaluate where we are, how we're doing, and what we need to do to keep our marriage alive.

Let yourself ask the questions. Rest assured that you will find new, convincing reasons to say:

Affirmation: I'd do it again.

We do not squabble, fight or row. We collect grudges.
                                        —Hugh Arnold

We keep track of each transgression, building a case on evidence collected over all the times we've been burned. As our list of grievances grows, we reach a simmer, then suddenly boil over.

It's better to talk about it before things reach the boiling point. Even the most heated arguments are more productive when dealt with in the present rather than allowing them to stew on the back burner.

Affirmation: It will only get hotter if I let it sit.

CHANGE

April 21

It doesn't much signify whom one marries, for one is sure to find out the next morning that it was someone else.
                    —Samuel Rogers

Some say that people never change, that the die is cast early and to think otherwise is to delude ourselves.

I disagree. Although it may not always be discernible, we are constantly in flux—our experiences alter our values, perceptions, and how we relate to each other.

Change and constancy are both essential to a successful marriage. If we can get excited about our mate's growth, as well as count on what's steady, we will feel stimulated *and* secure.

Affirmation: I will expect and embrace change.

SCENE FROM A MARRIAGE: You see her out of the corner of your eye. You should have known she'd be at the party; they were best friends long before you met him. She's wearing black. He's looking nervous. You wish you lived in another city. Can you ignore her? Or is this your chance to flaunt what you've got?

Neither.

Awkward as it is, this is your opportunity to be gracious.

What's past may be past, with the legacy ranging from friendly to frigid, but running into "the ex" is bound to bring up complicated feelings. You may like her, hate her, resent her, be grateful to her, or simply wish she didn't exist. All these feelings are normal. At the same time, depending on whether children are involved, you may have to deal with her on an ongoing basis.

To do so more easily, keep in mind these two important facts:

It's over.

He wants to be with you.

Affirmation: I am secure enough to be gracious.

PROJECTION

April 23

Nobody loves anyone the way he or she wants to be loved.
—Anonymous

We want our partner to express himself in the ways that make us feel wanted and loved. But *his* way isn't necessarily *our* way.

We want daisies, and he buys us a Dustbuster. We wait to be wined and dined; his idea of the perfect date is curling up on the couch, munching popcorn, and watching *The Simpsons*.

When we're all focused on getting what we want in exactly the way that to us spells L-O-V-E, we miss out on each other's genuine expressions of affection.

Affirmation: I will open myself to his way of loving.

I'm okay. You're a jerk.
            —*Anonymous*

This saying was going around after the book *I'm Okay, You're Okay* became a national best-seller.

Like all satire, it has an underlying ring of truth. We try in marriage to tune into our partner's "divine light" and act with Buddha-like acceptance; we try to adhere to the most sincere, most nonjudgmental self-help advice around when, deep down, we really think he's being a jerk.

Honesty, within limits, is refreshing. We do our marriage *more* good when we say what is, when we're willing to own the gap between altruistic ideals and our real—sometimes politically incorrect—feelings underneath.

Affirmation: It's okay to not always like each other.

April 25

Know that you have talent, are original, and have something important to say.
            —*Brenda Euland*

Brenda Euland was speaking to writers, but her words apply to all of us.

We must carry ourselves with confidence, knowing we bring talent and originality to our marriage. One may be wittier, the other a great masseuse, but each of us is equally gifted, with significant contributions to make.

The next time you feel the slightest bit insecure, meditate on this question: What is a most unique and wonderful thing about me? Then play from your strength.

Affirmation: I am one of a kind.

The greatest tragedy is indifference.
　　　　—Red Cross saying

"It doesn't matter," he shrugs when we push him to pick between the black-silk blazer and the purple-checked suit.

He's telling the truth. It *doesn't* matter to him! Which hardly means *you* don't matter or that your *feelings* don't matter!

Be careful not to interpret differences as indifference. Ask yourself, Are *you* always interested? Or are there parts of his life you couldn't care less about?

You can like different things in a marriage, but take pains to learn, respect, and admire what makes each other's heart sing.

Affirmation: I won't be indifferent if it matters to him.

PERSEVERANCE

April 27

Through each season, always.
> —Gary Stern

These words were engraved on my wedding ring.

Marriage has more seasons than winter, spring, summer, and fall. Seasons of hope and optimism, where everything seems right. Seasons of darkness, when we need to fight harder to live up to our commitment to love each other through it all.

The more seasons pass, the more we realize that our marriage is strong enough to weather the storms until the sun returns again.

Affirmation: Through rain and shine, I am with you.

It often takes more courage to change your opinion than to stick with it.

—*Georg Christoph Lichtenberg*

We get attached to our position, sometimes overstating it in order to convince ourselves *and* him that we're sure we know what we're talking about.

We'd do better to back off a bit. Instead of defending our opinions, we can open our minds and be willing to moderate our thinking. It *does* take courage to admit our platform isn't airtight. But it's also wonderfully freeing. After all, aren't two heads better than one?

Our perception is expanded when we can hear and understand each other's point of view.

Affirmation: Tell me what you think.

April 29

Five things not to say after turning out the light:
1. *"Honey, I've decided to become a Baptist."*
2. *"I hate it when you touch me there."*
3. *"Please don't take this as criticism."*
4. *"I put a tiny little dent in the Mercedes this morning."*
5. *"I want a divorce."*
   —*Robert Fulghum*

I know a couple on opposite time schedules. His day starts at seven A.M.; she gets up around noon and gets rolling around midnight.

They were fine as long as they got together in the early evening. But late-night fights disintegrated into crabby mornings and angry recriminations.

So they made a deal: Nothing heavy after ten P.M. If it was important enough, it needed to come up before. If not, it could be tabled until the next day.

Affirmation: It can wait.

I think the ideal relationship is good neighbors—you have your turf and he has his and you respect that.
    —Glenn Close

Notice that Glenn Close says "relationship," not "marriage."

Personally I'd rather learn how to live together than learn how to live well apart. Still, we do need to give each other space, whether it's separate corners in the house where we can be alone if we want or Tuesday nights when we each go out on our own.

We need to leave each other alone occasionally—*not* because we're angry, *not* because anything is wrong, but simply in order to be with ourselves.

Affirmation: We both need to be alone once in a while.

LISTENING

May 1

Unfortunately, sometimes people don't hear you until you scream.
> —*Stefanie Powers*

Married couples sometimes become "selectively hard of hearing." We tune out anything we'd rather not talk about, especially if it's static we've heard a million times before.

We crank up the volume when we sense our words are falling on deaf ears. We pout, scream, or stomp around until he takes the cotton out and starts responding.

We shouldn't have to work so hard to get his attention. We also shouldn't endlessly cover the same ground without regard for his feelings.

Make a deal: You'll think before you speak; he'll listen —and respond. If it's a prickly area, he'll take responsibility for either discussing it or tabling it to a later date. If it's a "broken record" conversation, you'll get off the needle.

Affirmation: I can speak softly and be heard.

"DON'T YOU KNOW WE USE HELLMANN'S, NOT KRAFT'S?!"

May 2

SCENE FROM A MARRIAGE: He starts to unpack the six overflowing grocery bags and pulls out the mayonnaise. Jeez! Can't he read!!! You spelled it out on the list— H-E-L-L-M-A-N-N-S. You don't care that he found a coupon for Kraft's on the floor!!! You wanted Hellmann's! What does it take to get him to follow orders?!

First of all, stop giving them. And that's an order!

Choosing the wrong brand is not grounds for a court-martial. You've forgotten this is a marriage, not the military, and sensitivity training is basic training for both of you.

It's your turn for a little attitude adjustment. You'll be in much better shape if you stop ordering him around and let go of your need to control. This doesn't mean grin and bear it; just try a softer approach.

If you think he's oblivious, let him know why it's important to you. If you think he's deliberately sabotaging you, find out why.

No matter what, remember to thank him for going to the store. Six bags is a lot of schlepping!

Affirmation: It's just mayonnaise.

SECURITY

May 3

I'm a locket in your pocket.
—Joey Morris

Recently I got upset when Joey made a casual coffee date with his old girlfriend, Kate. "It's nothing," he said, shrugging. "Oh, right! I'm sure she still has the hots for you," I said nastily, my insecurity creeping in past his repeated reassurances.

Then he said the thing about the locket. And my fear stopped dead in its tracks. Suddenly I realized I was simply jealous, that we all get jealous sometimes. No matter how secure we are in our relationship, we can still feel threatened when someone attractive appears on the scene.

The antidote is not to make him swear never to talk to another woman. No, it's up to us to have faith that we come first. That the love we hold for each other is a silver locket warm and safe in our pocket wherever we go.

Affirmation: I trust in your love.

Anyone who's a great kisser I'm always interested in.
—Cher

I don't know about you, but I put a high price on kissing. There's nothing like a good old-fashioned make-out scene in the car or on the couch to make us feel seventeen and head-over-heels in love again.

The art of kissing is easily neglected in the day-to-day of marriage. Perhaps once a year we should all go off on a bus to "Marriage Camp" with mandatory kissing sessions in between swimming and arts and crafts.

Or maybe we should just make a point of kissing our mate once, better yet several times a day.

Affirmation: Give me a kiss.

BAD DAYS

May 5

*Oh, life is a glorious cycle of song. A medley of extemporanea;
And love is a thing that can never go wrong. And I am Marie of
Roumania.*

                              —Dorothy Parker

So your marriage isn't turning out to be the Love Affair
of the Millennium. In fact there are times when instead of
"I do" you'd rather say, "I'm done."

That's okay. Although Dorothy Parker verges on the
cynical, her point is well taken: Life isn't always a song-
fest, and love can—and does—go wrong.

Which doesn't mean there's anything wrong with your
marriage. Bad days are simply part of the bargain. They
balance out the good days and help us appreciate the
times when, without any sarcasm, we can simply say:

Affirmation: I'm happy here.

A woman without a man is like a fish without a bicycle.
—*Gloria Steinem*

C'mon, Gloria! Men are good for more than that!

Even though it's funny, patronizing statements like this only serve to perpetuate the war between the sexes. Female presumptions of superiority push men away and prevent empathy and understanding.

It's time for us to work toward healing the split instead of widening it. Let's count all the ways his presence in our life enhances it.

Affirmation: I need him because:

1. _____.
2. _____.
3. _____.

May 7

Personally I think if a woman hasn't met the right man by the time she's twenty-four, she may be lucky.
—Deborah Kerr

Ten years ago women, on the average, got married at age twenty-two. Today that age has shot up to twenty-eight.

There are advantages to this. With age comes experience and hopefully some wisdom. We've spent more time getting to know ourselves and are better able to form healthy relationships. We're clearer about what we want and what we're able to give.

If you fall into the "older bride" category, know that maturity makes for all-around better mates—and heightens our capacity for appreciating the rightness of our relationship.

Affirmation: This was worth waiting for.

When he is late for dinner and I know he must be either having an affair or lying dead in the street, I always hope he's dead.
—Judith Viorst

No matter how secure we feel, we may still worry about our mate's fidelity. Especially when we aren't getting along wonderfully, it's easy to imagine the worst.

When we let our imagination run wild (TV talk shows are great fodder!), we create undue trouble for ourselves and our mate. Although there are no guarantees, the only way to have a peaceful and positive relationship is to assume our mate is totally trustworthy. Trust begets trust; if there's no real reason to worry, why worry?

Affirmation: I know I can trust you.

ATTENTIVENESS

I think the one lesson I have learned is that there is no substitute for paying attention.

—*Diane Sawyer*

When we rub his neck without being asked, that's paying attention. When he brings home Almond Sunset tea because he noticed us savoring it in the restaurant, that's paying attention. When we read between the lines and ask if he was hurt when his boss snubbed him at the Christmas party (even though he's acting cavalier), that's paying attention.

There is no substitute for it. Paying attention says, "You matter so much that I am aware of you at all times." It may be the single most important ingredient of a successful marriage.

Affirmation: You deserve my best attention.

Age does not protect you from love. But love, to some extent, protects you from age.
——*Jeanne Moreau*

Studies show that marriage is good for our health. Married men, especially, live longer on average than their unmarried counterparts.

Why is this? Perhaps being with another person forces us to take better care of ourselves, through diet, exercise, and relaxation. Perhaps because the affection we give and get keeps us feeling vibrant. Perhaps marriage motivates us to work on personal growth and well-being.

Or maybe love is restorative in and of itself.

Affirmation: Our love keeps me young.

May 11

*My true friends have always given me that supreme proof of
devotion, a spontaneous aversion for the man I loved.*
— Colette

It's great that our close friends understand what a jerk *he*
is—or how demanding *she* is.

Or is it?

On the one hand their loyalty is a gift. We know we
can tell them anything and count on their undying support.

On the other hand we set them—and ourselves—up.
When all we do is complain, we skew the picture, so they
can only see the flaws and aren't able to give us true
perspective.

It's great to have a sounding board, but it's equally
important for our friends to be the best fans of our marriage.

**Affirmation: True friends are supportive all
around.**

The ultimate lesson all of us have to learn is unconditional love, *which includes not only others but ourselves as well.*
—Elisabeth Kübler-Ross

In fact it begins with ourselves.

If we judge ourselves by rigid standards and withhold self-acceptance, we cannot unconditionally love and accept our mate.

His limitations remind us of our own. His all-too-human failings bring up the harsh, judgmental voice within that says, "It's not good enough. You'll have to do better if you want to be loved."

There is a different voice. We can say with conviction to ourselves—and our mate:

Affirmation: We are both fully and completely lovable.

POUTING

May 13

> *SCENE FROM A MARRIAGE: He's ignoring you again. Eyes glazed, staring at* Wheel of Fortune *while you try to talk to him. What does it take to get his attention? You pace back and forth, picking stuff up, muttering under your breath. You try the silent treatment. . . . three minutes . . . eight minutes . . . twelve minutes. . . . You turn off the TV. . . . He looks up and says, "What's going on?"*

What's going on is that you are sick to death of being ignored.

But passive-aggressive pouting won't help. Although there's a slight chance he'll notice and ask what's wrong, don't count on it. More likely you'll pout yourself right into despair and a full-blown standoff as he fails to take the bait.

So what's a girl to do? Either *blow up* or *back off.* An all-out tantrum is a more honest, direct way of getting his attention, although you run the risk of turning him off. Your other option is to wait until a better time, when you can claim his serious attention.

Affirmation: Don't just pout, do something about it.

There are couples who match and couples who clash.
—*Anonymous*

Have you noticed how some couples look like his/her pages in a catalog spread, while others look as mismatched as Bermuda shorts and a silk smoking jacket?

What I want to know is, are the L. L. Bean look-alikes, in twin workout gear and the black-booted bomber-jacket duos any more compatible, or do they just happen to have the same taste in clothes? Do contrasting styles truly clash, or do they make for an interesting, colorful blend?

We can look like a matched set without being coordinated. And we can cultivate distinctly different looks while remaining soul mates to the core. What matters is how we feel, not how we look.

Affirmation: Even if we look coordinated, we're cut from different cloth.

DEVOTION

*It's hard for me to keep my emotions inside. I want to express
them now. That's what a team is all about.*
                        —Earvin "Magic" Johnson

On November 5, 1991, much-loved basketball star Magic
Johnson held a press conference announcing the shocking
news that he is HIV-positive.

His wife of six months, "Cookie," was carrying their
first child. He says how smart he was to marry her. She
says she'll stand by him no matter what comes.

In sickness and in health, they are a team. "We'll fight
this together!" they vow.

Affirmation: We are playing for keeps.

I have sacrificed everything in my life that I consider precious in order to advance the political career of my husband.
—Pat Nixon

And why not?

If I were her, I might have tabled *my* career, too, in order to land both of us in the White House.

Like Pat we all make trade-offs. Unlike Pat most women no longer have the financial freedom to make such sacrifices, *nor* do we get anything close to First Lady perks as a result.

There are days we are grateful for the opportunity to advance our own career, on our own terms, and other days we wish we could give it up and be the "woman behind the man." In either case we need to be sure we never see ourselves as anything less than a total partner. We must give ourselves full credit for the energy, brains, and talent we put out, whether apart from him, for him, or beside him.

Affirmation: Every choice is fine, as long as we respect ourselves.

SECURITY

May 17

Who could really believe that there was some way to find protection in this world—or someone who could offer it?
       —Ann Beattie

Last night I had trouble sleeping. He was away, and I felt lonely. I wished I could cuddle up and wrap my arms around him so that I would feel safe.

Is this an illusion? Does marriage protect us, or are we each in fact alone?

In the largest sense there is no protection. Each of us is ultimately responsible for our own safety and security. But when raccoons scratch on the window in the middle of the night, it helps to have someone there, to shine a flashlight through the window and a light on our fears.

Affirmation: It helps to have you near me.

A man should kiss his wife's navel every day.
—Nell Kimball

Maybe that's going a little far.

On second thought, maybe not!

Is it too much to ask to be adored—shamelessly and with relish!

Why get married if not to enjoy the pleasure of having another human being treat us as if we are God's gift to humanity?

Let's make this promise: to never, ever take each other for granted.

Affirmation: I appreciate you.

PAIN

May 19

The pain of love is the pain of being alive. It's a perpetual wound.
—*Maureen Duffy*

Love opens us to the possibility of being hurt. It's like the country-western song that goes, "Love is a rose and you better not pick it . . ."

Love can be thorny and raw; it can also be fragrant as a rose. One of the greatest gifts of marriage is that we minister to each other's pain, as well as sweeten each other's lives.

Love hurts. It also heals.

Affirmation: I choose to feel alive and in love.

Cherish forever what makes you unique, cuz you're a yawn if it goes.

—Bette Midler

At first our differences are intriguing. She's into modern art, he's crazy about soccer. She dreams of going on safari, he cares deeply about the environment.

But before long we begin to merge. We nurture our common ground at the expense of cultivating our separate interests. Boredom sets in when we ignore the very things that define who we are—and what attracted us to each other in the first place.

Affirmation: I need to keep being me.

May 21

We need love and creative imagination to do constructive work.
—Paula Ollendorf

Love provides energy and motivation, the fuel that keeps us going even when the road is rough. Creative imagination is critical because every marriage needs unique strategies to overcome obstacles along the way.

Both are necessary tools. Neither is enough in and of itself.

Love makes it worthwhile. Creative imagination makes it possible.

Affirmation: We have the tools.

*SMART WOMEN KNOW . . . Sturm and drang make
for a good evening at the theatre, but not for a good relationship.*
—*Steven Carter and Julia Sokol*

If you are creating undue crisis in order to get a reaction
from your mate, stop! Instead, try to understand what it is
you want: his attention? interest? Even his anger may be
better than nothing if you feel him withdrawing.

Creating drama is one way to shake things up, but it
only results in a temporary storm. Once it dies down,
we're left with the aftermath.

Conflict is emotionally engaging. It creates a sense of
urgency and drama. Laughter, companionship, sex, and
serenity ultimately make for a more satisfying life together.

Affirmation: This is supposed to feel good.

RESPONSIBILITY

May 23

SCENE FROM A MARRIAGE: Sputter. Sputter. Sputter. The car rolls to a dead stop. You knew you should have pulled over at that Amoco station, but you were in such a hurry. You walk two blocks to a convenience store, call him at his office, and say, "Honey, you'll never believe what happened to me!"

He isn't amused.

In fact he's mad! How many times has he told you to fill up the tank, not just dribble in with whatever change you dig out of the bottom of your purse?

So he's right. You apologize. He tells you he's on a deadline. You apologize again. He says, "I guess I'll have to come and rescue you." You say, "Oh, forget it," and hang up on him.

Is this the only way this story can end?

Here's another scenario: He's right. You apologize. He tells you how busy he is, says he's really sorry but he cannot rescue you, and suggests you call the nearest gas station. You thank him for his help and take care of it yourself. And you learn from the experience.

Affirmation: We can help each other within reasonable limits.

For one human being to love another: that is perhaps the most difficult of all our tasks, the ultimate, the last test and proof, the work for which all other work is but preparation.
—*Rainer Maria Rilke*

This is why we are here on earth: to stretch and reach and become our best, most noble selves. To set aside our self-centered needs so as to reach a state of union and reunion.

The creative "work" of relationships is our most holy task. We knock ourselves out making a living, yet often neglect our real life's calling—that of loving another human being.

Marriage asks that we place our efforts where they are most deeply deserved.

Affirmation: I'm prepared to give my marriage my best.

FREEDOM

May 25

I can't mate in captivity.
　　　　　　　—Gloria Steinem

Sometimes we feel penned in by the proximity of marriage. Erotic desire is dampened by the day-to-dayness of sharing close quarters with our fellow-in-mate.

Time for a break. An afternoon apart—a haircut, lunch with a friend, or a browse through our favorite bookstore —helps to replenish energy and rekindle attraction and desire.

Here's another suggestion: Make a date with him. An hour before, have him leave the house while you bathe, perfume, and dress. Greet him at the door. See each other for the very first time.

Affirmation: I am not trapped.

It ain't over till it's over.
—*Yogi Berra*

At times we question our commitment. We wonder if it's time to throw in the towel. We ask ourselves, Is it still right? Is it still worth the effort?

How *do* you know?

You just know. You know it's worth it if you like who you are when you're with him. You know it's worth it if being with him enhances your health, sanity, and well-being. You know it's worth it if you feel incredibly grateful to have met him, even on the not-so-good days.

If some or all of the above is true, you're doing fine. If none of the above is true, you'll do yourself a favor to get professional help.

Affirmation: Until it's over, this relationship is worth working on.

May 27

Men don't get it!
—*Ellen Sue Stern*

What exactly do women *mean* when we say this? Just what is this mysterious "it" that men don't get?

We want them to understand our innermost feelings. We want them to care about what we care about. We want them to see the merits of different shades of lipstick. We want them to initiate meaningful conversation and clear the dishes without being asked.

Is this too much to expect?

Maybe not. But we have to be willing to work at it. If we patronize our mates, assuming they aren't educable, they'll simply resent our superior attitude and be less likely to try. If we really want understanding, we must approach our partners respectfully, asking for what we want, with patience and a willingness to explain just what "it" means.

Affirmation: I'm willing to spell it out.

Step Four: We conducted a fearless and searching moral inventory of ourselves.

—*from* Alcoholics Anonymous

Step Four of the Twelve Steps of Alcoholics Anonymous is not just meant for people involved in a formal recovery program; it is equally worthwhile for anyone in a committed relationship.

Marriage requires our willingness to conduct a rigorous inventory of our strengths and weaknesses. When we focus on ourselves, working on our "growing edges" instead of worrying about how our partner needs to change, we do our part in creating a healthy relationship based on mutual honesty and respect.

Affirmation: My personal growth is up to me. Yours is up to you.

May 29

They seemed to come suddenly upon happiness as if they had surprised a butterfly in the winter woods.
          —*Edith Wharton*

There are moments when we look at each other in utter surprise and delight, when we wonder what we ever did to deserve so much happiness.

At these moments we realize that marriage intensifies our capacity for joy. At these moments we recommit to noticing how truly wonderful life is. At these moments we get down on our knees and give thanks for the opportunity to give and receive love.

Affirmation: My heart is full.

An archeologist is the best husband any woman can have. The older she gets, the more interested he is in her.
—*Agatha Christie*

We worry about aging, squint our eyes in the mirror, search for crow's-feet and other signs that we're passing our prime.

We forget that he, too, gets older day by day. Like us he needs reassurance that we won't abandon him for a younger model, that our affection and attraction go way beyond his current physique.

If we can both be archeologists, willing to excavate and sift the sand for treasure, we will discover riches found only in the fullness of time.

Affirmation: I am willing to dig deep.

May 31

The basic discovery about any people is the discovery of the relationship between men and women.
—*Pearl S. Buck*

Here is one of the great challenges of marriage: to penetrate the mysterious qualities that both separate and attract women and men.

Every marriage is a single-handed experiment in cracking the mystery. We have the unique opportunity to bridge the gap—to transcend gender differences and develop true understanding of one another.

Over time, we come to appreciate the essential differences as well as learn how much we are really alike.

Affirmation: We are both different and the same.

June 1

One reason people get divorced is that they run out of gift ideas.
—*Robert Byrne*

We shop with a deep sense of purpose, searching for the perfect token of our affection, the object that expresses not only our love but an extraordinary understanding of our mate.

Too often our enjoyment is hampered by anxiety and the need for gratitude. We tell him twelve times how we spent our lunch hour combing obscure stores for the antique tie clip he admired three months ago. We wait for his exclamations of pleasure and appreciation and then wonder if he means it or is just trying to get the pressure off.

Enough! The old adage, It's the thought that counts, is true.

Affirmation: The act of giving is gift enough.

June 2

What is important is that one is capable of love. It is perhaps the only glimpse we are permitted of eternity.
—Helen Hayes

The expansiveness of love takes us beyond ourselves. Momentarily we feel as if we can fly, move mountains; we feel and want to live forever.

A glimpse of eternity gives us two precious commodities: hope and energy. In our enlarged vista we are filled with hope. *And* we have the energy to realize our vision.

What inspiring feelings! What a great opportunity to harness such emotion in the service of healing ourselves —and the planet.

Affirmation: I can see forever.

Don't smother each other. No one can grow in shade.
—Leo Buscaglia

Plants need sun and enough room to flourish.

So do people.

When we hover too close, acting overprotective or possessive, we block the light—and space—needed for personal growth.

Healthy nurturance requires a willingness to stand aside, allowing each other plenty of room to grow. Even when we *think* our partner is thirsty for love, advice, or support. Even when we're dying to take care of him.

Love is patient. Love waits for the right time.

Affirmation: I will step aside.

CLOSET SPACE

June 4

> *SCENE FROM A MARRIAGE: He used to have twelve hangers and three designated drawers. Now he's down to a darkened corner in the back of your overflowing closet. He flings your ever-multiplying articles of clothing right and left, getting more freaked out by the minute. It looks like the scene of a tornado. He retrieves his crumpled shirt from the bottom of a pile, looks at you disgustedly, and snorts, "You know, I live here too!"*

He's right. And you need to make some changes in order to be a respectful partner and roommate.

Physical space is both a concrete *and* a symbolic issue between spouses. You need to arrange your home so that there's room for both of your stuff. And you need to create a home in which both of you feel a sense of comfort and ownership.

Depending on your actual physical arrangements, you may choose to have separate closets. (It's saved more than one marriage!) If that's not possible, then you need to distribute the space fairly, and then make sure your clothes don't take over his side like alien beings in a science fiction movie.

Marriage is a good opportunity to clean up your act—and your closet! Start now!

Affirmation: Closet space is a great lesson in sharing.

A soft answer turneth away wrath.
　　　　　　　—*Proverbs 15:1*

There *will* be fights. You may have the most perfect marriage on the planet, but there will still come a time when you hurt each other, become angry, perhaps say words you wish you could take back.

In most cases a simple—yet very difficult—rule of thumb applies for reducing angry outbursts in marriage: If you can control your wrath, choosing your words carefully, uttering them softly, you may dissipate the rage enough to resolve the problem. Imagine saying, "I'm so mad, I could spit!" but in a whisper rather than a shout; we remove the edge while still getting our message across.

On the other hand there are situations that call for a powerful response. If you're being hurt, then say so, loudly and with conviction.

But first a distinction: There is hurt and there is harm. Occasional disappointment, sadness, or even pain comes with the territory.

However, abuse—emotional *or* physical—means it's time to rethink your relationship. It means it's time to speak up and get help.

Affirmation: I accept being hurt. I will never accept abuse.

June 6

Intimacy is not about that initial "Velcro stage" of relationships.
—Harriet Goldhur Lerner, Ph.D.

What a great way of describing the early, highly romantic stage when we first come together!

Velcro has two outstanding qualities: It's sticky (like falling in love, we get stuck on each other, we want to merge and be together constantly). And it's easy: the early stage of love is relatively smooth compared with the hard work of maintaining a relationship.

Yet, as Dr. Lerner says, ultimately we need to get beyond Velcro. Like a child learning to tie her shoes, we need to bridge the gap between our differences *and* we need to know how to hang in there when things get knotty.

Affirmation: The deeper ties of love take time.

The love we give away is the only love we keep.
—*Elbert Hubbard*

At times we feel as if we're giving more than we're getting. As if somehow the scales have tipped and we're getting the short end.

At these times it's important to ask why. Is your spouse distracted or lacking in emotional energy for a good reason? Do you actually *have* more to give at this moment, in which case why keep score?

In most marriages partners takes turns; first one is more generous, more giving, then the other. Of course if you're *always* the one giving, then you need to express your concern to your mate and ask him specifically for what you want.

Whatever you do, don't let your anger keep you from giving all the love *you* have to give.

Affirmation: When I give love, I get love.

June 8

Jesus said, "Love one another." He didn't say, "Love the whole world."
—*Mother Teresa*

Thank you, Mother Teresa.

For reminding us that marriage is a lesson in love. If we can reach beyond ourselves to our mate, that is enough.

Thank you for reminding us that caring deeply for one person at a time is the beginning of learning to love another—and another—until the world is filled with people who know how to be compassionate and loving.

So we needn't be overwhelmed. We need only begin in our own living room—with the one person with whom we have chosen to learn about love.

Affirmation: One person at a time.

I think self-awareness is probably the most important thing toward being a champion.
          —Billie Jean King

Acute awareness—the ability to be watchful and always on one's toes—makes for a champion in the game of tennis. No less so in the game of love.

In order to have a winning marriage, we need to pay concentrated attention to ourselves and our mates. We need to be conscious of who we are, what experiences have shaped us, and what really matters to us.

Then we can serve as well as receive.

Affirmation: The best score is Love–Love.

June 10

It is never too late to fall in love.
—*Sandy Wilson*

Couples complain that they've fallen out of love. The magic is gone. Their hearts have stopped pounding like a thousand conga drums; they no longer pine after each other when they're out of sight.

If this is happening to you, don't give up! Couples who have celebrated their first and fifth and twenty-fifth anniversary say that falling in love comes and goes, fading, then reappearing when we least expect.

Is there anything to help the process along? Sure! Intimate time together helps us recover romantic love. And so does time alone—luxuriating in a warm, candlelit bath; taking a solitary walk. Getting in touch with our innermost desires is key to rekindling romance.

Affirmation: The passion will return.

The first [principle] is always to begin where you are, not where you think you should be.
—Starhawk

We destroy ourselves with *should*s: I should be more fascinating, accomplished, and talented in order to keep my spouse interested for life! He should be more communicative, more understanding, more empathetic if we're ever going to have the kind of marriage I want.

Stop!!! If there's one *should*, it's this: We should accept exactly where each of us is *right now*.

When we pressure each other to be farther along, we feel defensive and angry: "Aren't I good enough as I am?!?" If we can begin with what's real—with who we are today—then we can lovingly move forward.

Affirmation: I accept where I am, I accept where you are.

CLEANING UP MESSES

June 12

> *SCENE FROM A MARRIAGE: You step out of bed right into a mess your puppy's left on the floor. He's sick as a dog (whoops! He is a dog!). Today's your sales presentation; everything's riding on it. You turn to your husband, who's due in court in ninety minutes, and say, "Wake up! We have to figure this out!"*

First, calm down. Neither panic nor anger (he hasn't said no yet) will help you solve the problem.

Now, let's figure this out. Here are the facts: The dog needs to go to the vet. You have to show up for work. He has to win his court case.

So far this looks pretty dismal. But wait! What time is your meeting? One o'clock. Great! He'll be out of court just in time to switch places so that you can dazzle your client.

Oh, that won't work? Okay. Plan B: Call your mother or mother-in-law. Reschedule your meeting for three. Call your best friend and beg. Call a vet who makes house calls—expensive but quick and worth it.

Why are *you* taking it all on? You're not. He'll make the calls while you shower, clean up the mess, and get dressed. Remember, this is marriage. Job-sharing and compromise are what it's all about.

Affirmation: We can work this out together.

To love without role, without power plays, is revolution.
   —Rita Mae Brown

As my children are fond of saying, "Women can do anything. Men can do anything . . . well, almost anything, except have babies."

Perhaps the day will come when even that is possible. In the meantime it behooves us all to seek absolute freedom for both men and women.

As we redefine traditional sex roles, marriage undergoes a revolution. No one dominates, no one gives up his or her essential being. Rather two people, equal in every respect, are free to become anything and everything we can be.

Affirmation: It's revolutionary—and romantic— for women and men to be absolutely equal.

COMMITMENT

June 14

All of a sudden you've decided that you "deserve" better. You are older, wiser, and better, but your spouse hasn't gotten any better. No problem. Just trade in the old one for a newer model.
—Rabbi Manis Friedman

I often hear people of my parents' generation say, "Kids these days don't understand commitment. They just stay married until they get bored or sick of it and then get divorced and marry someone else."

Not so. From what I can tell, people of our generation are seriously committed to making marriages work—both by hanging in there and by honestly confronting problems when they arise.

I don't see many people casually trading in their "old model," but rather making every effort to regularly tune up the one they've got.

Affirmation: My marriage deserves my absolute commitment.

Edith Bunker: "I was thinking. In all the years we've been married, you never once said you was sorry."

Archie Bunker: "I'll gladly say I'm sorry—if I ever say anything wrong."

Perfect Archie Bunker! The irony being that he's absolutely sincere—as are most of us in our blindness to our faults and owning up when we're in the wrong.

Even when we know we've erred, we may choke on the words *I'm sorry,* worried they're not enough to make a difference.

But they do. The other side is graciously to accept our mate's apologies, letting him know we appreciate what it takes to swallow his pride.

Affirmation: I make mistakes. I make amends.

HOLINESS

June 16

You are God's work of art.
—Saint Paul

We should admire our beloved as an original creation, specially designed by the most talented sculptor that ever existed.

When we look deep inside, we come in touch with the holiness inherent in every human being. We can clearly see our mate's absolute perfection as well as our own. Then we gaze on each other with the awe and appreciation befitting a classic work of art.

Affirmation: I stand before you awed by your beauty.

I love you. And it's getting worse.
                    —*Joseph Morris*

Joey turned to me and said this about three months into our already tumultuous relationship.

We both laughed. And we both knew what he meant.

Sometimes being in love is exhausting. The process of opening ourselves and getting to know another person—his tastes, his quirks, his complicated psyche—can seem like more than we bargained for.

Yet we hang in there.

Why?

Because the ecstasy exceeds the effort. Because, deep down, we know we belong together.

Affirmation: I love you. And it's getting worse.

LISTENING

The first duty of love is to listen.
                    —Paul Tillich

Just listen.

It's that simple. Which doesn't mean it's easy.

Real listening requires more than a token nod or interpreting what's said through our own experience. Listening requires real concentration and the willingness to silence our inner voice. It requires taking in another person's thoughts and feelings without agreeing, disagreeing, or pretending to completely understand.

When we feel heard, we feel loved.

Affirmation: My ears and my heart are open.

Now we have history as well as chemistry.
                                    —*Anna Quindlen*

I really like this distinction between a short-term affair and a long-term relationship.

Anna Quindlen goes on to say, "An enormous part of my past does not exist without my husband." That shared past—storms weathered, children grown, holidays come and gone—deepens our love and attraction.

Chemistry draws us together; history weaves us together. In time we become each other's reference point, each other's family.

Affirmation: We are memories in the making.

AGING

June 20

It seems the older men get, the younger their new wives get.
—Elizabeth Taylor

She should talk! After her much-publicized marriage to forty-year-old Larry Fortensky, twenty years her junior.

Age needn't be a deciding factor in whom we love; today both women and men feel freer to pursue autumn-spring romances. Which is great! As long as we don't trade in our old spouse for a newer model as a way of warding off mortality and reclaiming our youth.

As we age, our partner mirrors our own decline. Our partner *also* mirrors the growing beauty that comes with maturity.

Affirmation: Let us ripen together

"WE DON'T NEED A NEW TOASTER OVEN!"

SCENE FROM A MARRIAGE: Money's tight, and you already have a microwave. You really needed that holiday bonus to buy Christmas gifts for your family. Aren't you supposed to check with each other before running off and charging things? Who's running the show around here?

You both are. And *that's* one of the biggest challenges of managing money in a marriage.

Money (along with sex) is nearly always a loaded issue between couples. How we make it, spend it—on what and why—is at minimum a point of negotiation and can be a source of conflict, bringing up questions of values, power, and differences in upbringing.

You're likely to bang heads on this one. Here are a few rules to prevent marriage-money-migraines:

1. Agree on a modest discretionary budget for individual purchases.
2. Agree to discuss purchases over a certain dollar amount.
3. Accept that you *will* have differences over money, which has little to do with love or compatibility.

Affirmation: Negotiating money matters is one way of learning to be healthy partners.

RESPONSIBILITY

June 22

You become responsible forever, for what you have tamed. You are responsible for your rose.
—Antoine de Saint-Exupéry

Have you ever watched a professional lion tamer? You can see the incredible patience and respect that has gone into nurturing such a potentially volatile relationship.

How is this accomplished? Through commitment and responsibility: commitment to do whatever it takes to earn trust; responsibility to be utterly respectful, to watch and listen and learn the meaning of every move.

So it is with our spouse. We tame each other, not by yielding power but, little by little, by building trust and respect.

Affirmation: I am responsible to my beloved.

At the touch of love, everyone becomes a poet.
                              —*Plato*

Even if our affection isn't manifested in the actual making of "art," the experience of loving inspires us to be our most creative selves. The world appears more vivid; we are moved to express what's in our hearts, and surprisingly it sounds like poetry.

   That's why we write love letters, to sing the poetry inside our soul sparked by the touch of love.

Affirmation: Art is an expression of love.

June 24

If you are all wrapped up in yourself, you are overdressed.
—Kate Halverson

Marriage gives us the opportunity to wrestle with our perfectly human self-absorption. We're forced to consider another person equally, to draw the focus away from our own drama and pay attention to our spouse's feelings and needs.

This can get confusing. How do we know when to assert our needs and when to set them aside to accommodate our mate?

We know by how we feel. When we are confident and secure, we can remove outer layers of protective covering and let another person in. When we feel resentful, we need to check and make sure we're "dressed" comfortably. If not, it's time to cover ourselves until we're warm enough to give.

Affirmation: Marriage means undressing, in more than one way.

What do we live for, if it is not to make life less difficult for each other?

—*George Eliot*

That *is* the point, isn't it?

Marriage gives us a lot, but asks a great deal too. Going out of our way to help each other, to soften hard times and lend support is part of the obligation—and the privilege—of matrimony.

To lessen each other's load is one way of saying, "I love you." I love you enough to extend myself. I care enough to try to make life easier for you.

Affirmation: How can I help you?

June 26

No partner in a love relationship should feel that he has to give up an essential part of himself in order to make it viable.
—May Sarton

Marriage takes a lot of work. We feel pressured to adapt to our partner's expectations; he won't play the accordion when we're around for fear of our ridicule; we know he'd like someone less intense, so we censor ourselves, being careful not to overwhelm him.

Slowly we cut off the corners of who we are in order to be loved. This is a bad idea. We don't have to adore everything about our spouse, but we do have to allow, accept, and whenever possible affirm one another.

Affirmation: No cutting corners.

When I look into the future, it's so bright, it burns my eyes.
—*Oprah Winfrey*

Yes!!!

This is how it feels when we first say "I do." And this is what it means to feel right about our marriage. The horizon is brilliant, with infinite potential. We are energized and inspired, ready to take on the world!

Let us look together into the burning future, anticipating a shared future filled with happiness and peace.

Affirmation: I'm excited.

IMAGINATION

June 28

If the only tool you have is a hammer, you tend to think of every problem as a nail.
—*Abraham Maslow*

Too often we get stuck in a rut, pounding away with one particular approach to problem solving. We process endlessly when a long hug would go a lot farther. We're rational when we should be calling the tools of the heart into play.

We need lots of different options and strategies. Sometimes simply changing our approach shakes things up enough to give us a whole new perspective.

Affirmation: If it isn't working, change it.

One of the secrets of a long and fruitful life is to forgive everybody every night before you go to bed.
      —*Anonymous (Quoted by Ann Landers)*

This is perfect advice for a long and fruitful marriage.

Each night we can wipe the slate clean; each morning we can begin the new day with resolve to do a better job of loving. (And if it takes a few days, that's okay, too!)

The goal is to remember that none of us is perfect and to be able to say to ourselves and to each other:

Affirmation: Tomorrow is another day.

"ARE YOU *EVER* GOING TO GET OFF THE PHONE?"

June 30

> SCENE FROM A MARRIAGE: *It's been forty-five minutes and you're* still *on the phone. It's your best friend and she's had an awful fight with her husband. She needs you!!! Meanwhile your husband's getting pissed off. You promised to watch a movie with him and it's getting late. He's glaring at you. She's talking to you. What are you going to do?*

Get off the phone!

Yes, I know she's your best friend. But are you willing to fix her marriage at the expense of messing up your own? Unless this is a matter of life or death (and few things are), forty-five minutes is plenty of time. If it isn't, she needs a therapist, not a friend.

Meanwhile *you* need to stop jeopardizing your marriage by putting her ahead of your husband. And you need to be aware of how you're using the phone—and your connection to your friend—as an intimacy stopper.

If you have to, take it off the hook or put on your answering machine. Whatever it takes to tune in to your marriage.

Affirmation: I'm off the phone.

Despite my thirty years of research into the feminine soul, I have not yet been able to answer . . . what does a woman want?
—*Sigmund Freud*

Most men would say the same.

But that doesn't mean we should throw up our hands, heave a great sigh, and stop trying to comprehend these mysterious differences.

On the contrary, what's called for is earnest communication—asking, What do you want?

We can listen and strive to understand and interpret what is meant, then do what we can to help one another realize our heart's desire.

Affirmation: I want to know what you want.

APPRECIATION

July 2

My mother was dead for five years before I realized that I loved her very much.
—Lillian Hellman

Oh, why does it take losing—or almost losing—our beloved before we truly appreciate each other?

The time to feel and express our love is now. In the present. When we have the chance to take our beloved's hand in our own, wrap our arms around him, or simply look in his eyes and know how very, very lucky we are to share each other's life.

Let us never look back in regret having neglected to say the words:

Affirmation: I love you.

He is a man whom it is impossible to please because he is never pleased with himself.
—*Johann Wolfgang von Goethe*

Some of us live with a partner who is critical or judgmental; nothing is ever good enough, right enough, perfect enough. So we knock ourselves out trying to please, never able to accomplish the impossible.

That's because it *is* impossible. Until we can reconcile our humanity, no one can live with a partner's perfectly human limitations. Compassion begins with ourselves.

Affirmation: I can only live up to my own expectations.

FREEDOM

July 4

I like the dreams of the future better than the history of the past.
—Thomas Jefferson

Apt words on Independence Day from one of our country's founders.

And what a good attitude with which to proceed in marriage. To keep our eye fixed firmly on a vision of what may lie ahead. To continually integrate the history we've shared as a foundation for future growth in our relationship with our mate.

Today is a day to remember our best dreams—in all their sparkling brilliance—and to give thanks for the precious gift of freedom to make them happen.

Affirmation: Together we dream the future into being.

One advantage of marriage, it seems to me, is that when you fall out of love with him, or he falls out of love with you, it keeps you together until you maybe fall in love again.
—Judith Viorst

I knew a couple who got engaged two weeks into their courtship. After ten years of marriage, sometimes smooth, sometimes rocky, he still insists that proposing quickly was the right thing to do—it ensured that they'd stick together and work things out when the going got tough.

This is certainly one way to look at it. Commitment keeps us in, even when we fantasize about getting out. We turn our wedding ring over and over on our finger, recalling our vows, remembering the deep feelings of love and destiny that moved us to say, "I do."

If, at this particular juncture, the best you can say is, "I do commit to stay in," that's enough for now. In marriage, as in life, things change by the moment. Without commitment, we might tragically leave just a moment too soon.

Affirmation: I'm here right now.

CONFLICT

July 6

Too much agreement kills a chat.
                    —Eldridge Cleaver

Disagreement—even over important issues—makes for lively dialogue.

Don't let it scare you; we needn't see eye-to-eye. On the contrary, holding differing opinions—the more feisty the better—keeps things interesting and exciting.

Personally I pray that the "Yes, dear" days are over forever. When we're truly in agreement, great. When we're not, let's talk, spar, even passionately fight it out until we can say with conviction:

Affirmation: I see your point of view.

Love doesn't just sit there, like a stone; it has to be made, like bread, remade all the time, made new.
—*Ursula K. Le Guin*

We cannot allow our relationship to stagnate and expect it to remain nourishing.

Even the hottest love affairs can cool and turn stale. We must continually add fresh yeast, patiently knead, and wait and watch until the moment comes when we can break bread, fresh and fragrant, together.

There is no rushing it. No saving it. Each day we rise and make love again.

Affirmation: Our love is alive and ever-changing.

MONOGAMY

July 8

I've looked at a lot of women with lust. I've committed adultery in my heart many times.
—Jimmy Carter

No problem. Although former president Jimmy Carter created a minor scandal with this quote from a *Playboy* interview, I think he said what's true for most, if not all of us.

Let's face it, the world is full of beautiful, interesting, and sexy people. There's nothing wrong with looking, so long as we don't touch or break anything precious, particularly our commitment to our mate.

Think of it as window-shopping—we appreciate the finery without spending a dime.

Affirmation: Just looking.

It's never too late to have a happy childhood.
      —Anonymous

Marriage offers a unique opportunity to heal the wounds of the past and learn to be a happier person.

Each of us brings unfinished business into our relationship—insecurities over being a fat teenager, a father who ignored us, our parents' divorce—which makes it difficult to fully trust that we will make it as a couple forever.

We must deal with our old issues or they will come up in our marriage. It is up to us to heal—whether we write in a journal, see a therapist, or simply talk it over with a friend. When we clear out the past, we are more fully alive and able to love in the present.

Affirmation: I can be a happy and peaceful adult.

ISOLATION

July 10

Loneliness and the feeling of being unwanted is the most terrible poverty.

> —*Mother Teresa*

Imagine the poverty she's seen.

Yet Mother Teresa knows there is no greater impoverishment than feeling alone and unwanted.

Sometimes we feel most isolated with another person right beside us. We feel paralyzed to reach out. We just don't know how to bridge the gap.

When we feel as if there's a wall between us, we must do two things: *say so* (the truth always brings a degree of peace) and *ask for what we need* (a hug or simple words of reassurance).

Affirmation: I am with you.

Remember! You're two different animals. Men and women cannot totally unite.

—Pierre Mornell

Is this true?

Sometimes it seems that way. Times when we could use a Berlitz crash course to understand what in the world he's talking about. Times when, for the life of us, we can't figure out how to reach him or why we'd even want to.

Other times we seem like kindred spirits. We come together effortlessly; he feels like our male counterpart—twin, brother, friend, and lover with whom we experience a deep, sustaining connection.

Both are true. Both make marriage profoundly energizing.

Affirmation: We are more alike than different.

THE ANNIVERSARY

July 12

> *SCENE FROM A MARRIAGE:* You're rounding the corner on a year. You want to celebrate. You want to mark this important milestone in your life. You've always imagined a romantic candlelit dinner at a fancy restaurant, exchanging expensive gifts, toasting another year of marriage. You make a reservation at the restaurant where you had your first date. You tell him. He pauses, looks embarrassed, then says, "Money's tight, honey. Can't we just stay home?"

Yes. The answer is yes.

Being together at home is far more important than spending money you don't have doing the town.

Besides, you can still create the perfect romantic evening. Music, candles, maybe dinner in bed, just the two of you, is cozier and more intimate than sharing your night with a roomful of strangers.

As far as gifts go, a small, meaningful present is every bit—maybe more—romantic than an elaborate, expensive offering. A beautiful card with a heartfelt message will be deeply appreciated.

Down the road you may someday have the means to celebrate in style. But you will always remember your first anniversary, money scarce, love abundant, the future full of promise.

Affirmation: Happy anniversary.

When we look at him, we don't see who he is right now. He's not just Jerry, but Jerry-who-never-shows-up-on-time-for-dinner, or Peter-who-takes-me-for-granted, or Andrew-who-wouldn't-stand-up-to-my-father.
—Ellen Sue Stern

Images accumulate over time; a pile of past experiences shape our perceptions and cloud our capacity to see each other clearly in the present.

Every so often we need to update our images. So that we can appreciate the very real ways in which we've changed and grown. So that we can relate to each other as dynamic works-in-progress rather than finished products.

To do so requires letting go of past anger and disappointment. It requires a fresh mind and a fresh heart, open to who our mate is becoming right now, today.

Affirmation: It's time to let go of old tapes and give him the benefit of the doubt.

MIND-SET

Words to eliminate: impossible
 can't
 if only . . .
—*Gerald G. Jampolsky, M.D.*

How we *think* powerfully affects how we *feel* toward our mate.

If we think it's impossible to work out problems, then it is. If we *think* we can't be worthy of our partner's respect, then we never will be. If we *think* our marriage would be better if only we had more money . . . if only he'd send flowers . . . then we spend our whole lives waiting for what will never come.

Instead we can replace our fear-based thinking with positive words:

Affirmation: It's possible. We can. Right now.

Somebody's boring me—I think it's me.
　　　　　　　　　—*Dylan Thomas*

When we're bored or unhappy, we yawn in the direction of our spouse, wishing he was more stimulating.

We're yawning at the wrong person. Most likely we're bored with ourselves. This is a sign that it's time to expand our interests, see close friends or make new ones, reevaluate what matters to us and where we're investing our energy.

It's amazing, once we regenerate ourselves, how exciting our mate can be.

Affirmation: I'm responsible for entertaining myself.

SEX

Alvie: "We hardly ever have sex . . . about three times a
week."

Annie: "We always have sex . . . about three times a
week."

—*Woody Allen*

This dialogue from the movie *Annie Hall* beautifully cap-
tures what goes on behind closed doors.

It's rare for our libidos to be perfectly matched. So
many factors affect sexual desire at any given moment—
our health, whether our weight is up or down, what kind
of day we've had at work.

But that doesn't keep us from taking it personally when
one wants it and the other doesn't.

So what can we do when we're sexually out of sync?
First, don't panic. Then, look at whether the disparity is
situational or reflects an emotional trend that needs to be
addressed. If so, deal with it. If not, grab a good book,
give each other a kiss good night, and know that:

Affirmation: There will be another week.

Power is the ultimate aphrodisiac.
　　　　　—Henry Kissinger

Power *is* sexy!

We're attracted to each other's confidence and savvy in the world.

Great stuff. But we need to balance this with an appreciation of softness and vulnerability.

We all have days when we feel on top of the world, and others when we need lots of reassurance. Let's be turned on to each other when we're hot. And when we're not.

Affirmation: You don't have to be on to impress me.

COURAGE

July 18

Life shrinks or expands in proportion to one's courage.
— *Anaïs Nin*

It takes great courage to experience true intimacy with another human being. The bravery to reveal our inner selves. The bravery to confront the barriers—real and imagined—that keep us from loving and letting ourselves be loved. The bravery to summon will and effort when required, as well as to allow ourselves to surrender when that's what's called for.

There is no greater courage. And there is nothing that stretches us so far, expanding our hearts, our vision, and the quality of our lives.

Affirmation: My life is expanding.

It is not who is right, but what *is right that is important.*
—*Thomas Huxley*

Being right provides limited rewards. We enjoy a momentary surge of power and achievement, but alas, sweet victory is short-lived, especially if we leave our partner in the bitter throes of defeat.

By contrast, when we are mutually committed to a process of discovery, the pursuit of truth is deeply fulfilling. When we dedicate ourselves to a shared journey of finding *what* is right, rather than *who* is right, then we struggle *with* rather than against each other.

The latter is a far nobler goal—and a far better way to travel.

Affirmation: Let's learn together.

KVETCHING

July 20

I personally think we developed language because of our deep inner need to complain.
—*Lily Tomlin in* The Search for Signs of Intelligent Life in the Universe, *by Jane Wagner*

In her one-woman production, Lily Tomlin's bag-lady character, Trudy, struggles to discover the evolutionary roots of language.

I think she's on to something. We *do* like to complain. As a rule, we're more cognizant of what's missing in our lives—and in our marriages—than what's worthy of celebration.

Make a point of being aware of how often you complain. An experiment: Notice the next five times you kvetch about your mate or your marriage. Each time stop and ask yourself, *Is this really an issue?* If it is, stop moaning and do something about it! If not, try putting into words your gratitude and pleasure.

Affirmation: I have a deep inner need to be happy.

Three things in human life are important. The first is to be kind. The second is to be kind. The third is to be kind.
—*Elbert Hubbard*

This quote makes me want to call each and every person I love and say something nice—a compliment or thank you or an offer to help in some way that would add peace and pleasure to their lives.

This is what loving is about—being kind to one another. Let's cut the sarcasm and judgments and tread gently, carefully, with great consideration for each other's feelings.

Affirmation: Kindness is akin to love.

TAKING OUT THE GARBAGE

July 22

SCENE FROM A MARRIAGE: You've asked five times. Nicely. You'd like to scream. You'd like to threaten. You've emptied it, tied it up, and left it by the door. You've had it. You march across the room, sling the green Hefty bag over your shoulder, lug it out to the garage, and dump it in the driver's seat of his car.

Good for you!

Or is it?

Sometimes we need to grandstand, especially if nothing else seems to work. Although this high-risk strategy is effective in making a statement—a strong statement!—it doesn't address the real issue: how to work out an equitable division of labor.

Getting his attention, whatever it takes, is a first step. The next step is to cool down and negotiate realistic commitments. (One piece of advice: Take turns taking out the garbage—it's not the best job in the house.)

Affirmation: I'll save throwing scenes for when it's absolutely necessary.

Whenever I blow it, I worry that he won't love me anymore.
—*Anonymous*

When we screw up, we get stuck in our own shame. When we let ourselves and our mate down, we feel trapped, as if there's no way out of the mess we've made.

But there is a way out. Here are the magic words:

"I'm sorry. What can I do to make it better?"

That's all any of us can do. To apologize, mean it, and make every effort to repair the damage.

Affirmation: I'm sorry.

CONTROL

July 24

It's the effort, not the outcome that counts.
                                    —*Anonymous*

We needn't be perfect. We needn't even come close.

What matters is to do our best job at being giving and present in our marriage.

When we do so and it doesn't achieve the desired outcome (I surprised him with a candlelit dinner and all he talked about was what a jerk some guy was at work), we need to let go of our need to control. We need to compliment ourselves for *our* effort, for being our best selves in the relationship, irregardless of how he acts or what he does or doesn't give back.

Otherwise we make ourselves crazy.

Affirmation: I can only control what I do.

When it is dark enough, you can see the stars.
    —*Charles Beard*

There are times when we feel like giving up, when we feel beaten and hopeless and wonder why we bother at all.

That's when we need faith. Faith is what separates marriages that make it from marriages that crumble. Faith that we have the courage and wherewithal. Faith that our love will carry us through the darkest nights.

In the aftermath of struggling with difficult and painful issues, we feel renewed hope. We look up and count the stars.

Affirmation: Darkness isn't the absence of light.

PERSPECTIVE

July 26

Angels can fly because they take themselves lightly.
—G. K. Chesterton

We weigh ourselves down when we take ourselves too seriously, when we lose sight of the big picture and become overly invested in the drama of our lives.

We need to release our burdens, if even for a moment. We free ourselves when we can step back and remember that we are but one small part of a vast universe, no more, no less than the birds and the angels flying all around us.

Affirmation: I can lighten up and still take my life seriously.

I take care of me. I'm the only one I've got.
—Groucho Marx

We all need to take care of ourselves; that's what it means to be a grown-up capable of an adult love relationship.

Which doesn't mean we have to do it all on our own. There's a big difference between dependence and depending on each other. Being able to say, "I need you," means "I trust you enough to be vulnerable—to care for you and allow you to care for me."

Each of us stands on our own two feet. Being married means we link arms and make sure neither of us takes a fall.

Affirmation: I'm independent enough to depend on you.

SELF-RESTRAINT

July 28

Intimacy is tempered by lightness of touch.
    —*Anne Morrow Lindbergh*

It's a natural impulse to hold on harder when he pulls away. To get scared—even panicky—that his interest is fading, that he's bored or no longer in love.

Fear and desperation drive us to be heavy-handed. It's suddenly life-or-death that he share his feelings, even though he'd rather keep them to himself. We back him into a corner as if we suspect he's a double agent about to confess that he's heading back out into the cold.

To say the least, all this might push him away—when all he needed was a moment's respite from the intensity of interacting. A little distance needn't mean the intimacy has died. If we can tread more lightly, he'll come toward us when he's ready.

Affirmation: There is plenty of room and plenty of time.

Always tell the truth—it's the easiest thing to remember.
—David Mamet

Even if it's only a little white lie, we trip ourselves up when we veer away from the truth.

Honesty is the first commandment of marriage. Without it there can be no trust. Without it we can never be sure of where we stand with our mate.

Sometimes it's hard to be honest. We're tempted to bend the truth in order to protect ourselves and avoid an uncomfortable confrontation.

But honesty, no matter how painful, is an act of love and self-respect. It expresses our regard for our mate and our belief that we are both mature adults capable of facing the truth.

Affirmation: We are strong enough to deal with what's real.

"WHAT DO YOU MEAN, YOU DIDN'T ASK FOR THE RAISE?"

July 30

> *SCENE FROM A MARRIAGE: You've been waiting on pins and needles all day. That extra money is just what you need to make ends meet. He walks in from work and turns on the news. "So?" you say, not even trying to hide your impatience. "So what?" he responds. "So, did you get it?" you try again. "Get what?" he says, flipping the station with the remote control.*

How can you live with someone who doesn't even have the balls to ask for the raise he's worked so hard for and deserves so much?!

Maybe you should have married someone more ambitious. More aggressive. More worldly-wise.

And now what are *you* supposed to do? Just shut up and accept things as they are?

Okay. Cool off. How about a compromise? Gently (I said, gently) ask what happened. Don't judge. Don't criticize. See if you can help plan for another opportunity for him to approach his boss.

In the meantime take all that ambition, aggression, and savvy you're overflowing with and do what *you* can to get ahead.

Affirmation: Sometimes I have to believe in him and back off.

Marriage resembles a pair of shears, so joined that they cannot be separated, often moving in opposite directions, yet always punishing anyone who comes between them.
—Sydney Smith

Remember when you used to complain about your mother, but when your best friend chimed in, you immediately got mad?

That's how we feel about our mate. We can analyze, criticize, even trash him to our friends, but if they say anything bad—watch out!

Although this may seem hypocritical, loyalty plays an important role in keeping marriage strong. We need to know we can depend on each other's support. We need confidence that our partner will stand up for us, no matter how privately aggravated we might be at any given moment.

Loyalty builds solidarity. Solidarity builds trust. And trust makes marriage a sanctuary.

Affirmation: I'm with you.

ROLES

A house does not need a wife any more than it does a husband.
—Charlotte Perkins Gilman

Time was when being a "good wife" was synonymous with making the pages of *House Beautiful*.

The times they are a-changing!

Today husbands *and* wives share responsibility for the home we make together. Although we still have some distance to go (according to a recent survey, women continue to take on eighty percent of domestic tasks), at least we no longer automatically assume housekeeping to be exclusively women's work.

Today we have the freedom to negotiate domestic responsibilities in whatever way makes sense, from job-sharing, to hiring help, to one partner working outside the home while the other works within.

Anything goes—as long as all work has equal value.

Affirmation: We are both working hard and giving what we can.

August 2

Trying to help an oppressed person is like trying to put your arms around someone with a sunburn.
　　　　　　　　　—Florynce Kennedy

There are times when our mate is unapproachable. We've had a fight. Or his father has blown up at him. Or he's just crabby or anxious or in a bad mood for no apparent reason.

When we see him this way, we want to *do* something! We want to fix it by talking things through or putting our arms around him.

That's what *we* need. It may not be what *he* needs right then.

Give him a little time. Time to recover his self-esteem. Time to let go of his shame or embarrassment. Time to open his arms when *he's* ready to accept your comfort.

Affirmation: I'll wait until the right moment.

FEEDBACK

August 3

PRINCIPLE 1: *Most of your partner's criticisms of you have some basis in reality.*
—*Harville Hendrix*

Criticism usually makes us defensive. We feel exposed and start to fend off what seems like an attack.

Hard as it is, we have another option. We can swallow our pride, listen, and try to accept our partner's criticism as helpful feedback. We can assume he is coming from a place of love rather than assuming he's out to get us.

We have much to gain if we can allow our mate to be a teacher—once in a while—and trust his intent to help us know ourselves better.

Affirmation: I trust that my partner has my best interests in mind.

In a good vegetable soup the onion is not constantly sticking up its head for extra attention and yelling, "I'm the onion, I'm the onion." . . . It is contributing with the other vegetables to the good flavor of the soup.

—Natalie Goldberg

Great marriages are a blend; we each bring flavorful ingredients, and the soup gets better and better to eat.

After a while we don't recall who threw in what. The great sense of humor that's saved many an argument from escalating into a full-scale battle keeps the temperature right. The exquisite sensitivity adds tenderness. The level-headedness that we've come to depend on—terrific in moments of crisis—keeps the soup from boiling over.

Every ingredient adds something.

Affirmation: We each add so much nourishment to our marriage.

COHABITATION

August 5

Most of us can't live peacefully with ourselves, let alone with someone else.

—*Sy Safransky*

No kidding!

It's hard enough to live with our own constantly changing moods without having to put up with the same —or worse—from another human being.

But that's part of what marriage is about. Learning to live with each other when it's a breeze as well as when it's a drag. Being together even when we're in sad shape. Reading signals; knowing when to come close and when to get out of the way.

Remember, being roommates isn't always about being in the same place at the same time.

Affirmation: Slowly we will learn to live together.

SCENE FROM A MARRIAGE: It's been the most wonderful day! You snuggled and read the paper together . . . went out for brunch . . . saw a movie . . . or talked about the beautiful children you'll have someday . . . and made mad, passionate love. Does it get any better than this?

Remember this feeling!

Sometimes—hopefully lots of times—being married will be like a beautiful dream filled with all the things you've ever wanted.

You feel peaceful. Joyous. Grateful for the opportunity to spend the rest of your life with this incredible person.

You may also wait for the other shoe to drop. After all, this can't go on, can it?

Sure. Although every day won't be quite so dreamy, your feelings of peace, joy, and gratitude are available to you at all times.

Affirmation: I will savor this feeling.

COMPANIONSHIP

August 7

People who get married because they're in love make a ridiculous mistake. It makes much more sense to marry your best friend.
—*Fran Lebowitz*

Oh, such a cynic! And yet there is a germ of truth in what she says.

We need both passion and friendship to make our marriage a success. Passion is a hot flame, but friendship is the bedrock that sustains.

Being in love makes us want to be totally here *right now,* inspired to give beyond what we ever imagined possible.

Friendship grounds us over the long haul, motivating us to be there through thick and thin, even in moments when we feel more loving than in love.

Affirmation: I want to be your friend and your lover.

August 8

Love is the most subtle form of self-interest.
—Holbrook Jackson

Love needn't pretend to be altruistic. It's just fine for partners to benefit individually from the arrangement of marriage; it's just fine to love our mate and want to be with him in part because doing so gives us things we want for ourselves.

Reciprocity isn't selfish so long as we are clear about what we give and what we get, so long as our love is mutual and isn't manipulative or dishonest in any way.

Affirmation: I care about what each of us gets from our marriage.

HONESTY

I am never afraid of what I know.
        —Anna Sewell

Not knowing is the worst. When we're in the dark about our spouse's feelings, worrying what his silence means or whether he's still attracted to us, we feel frightened. We fantasize the worst. What we imagine is often more sinister than what the truth holds.

Yet we hesitate to ask, for fear that we won't be able to cope with the answers.

Whatever is, is. Trust that you can—and will—be able to handle anything that comes up, as long as you know where you stand.

Affirmation: What I know about I can deal with.

It is harder to kill a phantom than a reality.
—Virginia Woolf

We all come into marriage with ghosts; they haunt us and limit our capacity to be intimate.

Whether it's the ex-girlfriend, the abusive parent, or the job of a lifetime that got away, whatever's unresolved from the past negatively affects the quality of our relationship.

We must make a concerted effort to face the past so that we can be fully present with our mate. Here are four ways to go phantom hunting:

1. Write in a journal.
2. See a therapist or counselor.
3. Go back and honestly confront your pain—either with the individual who was part of it or on your own.
4. Seek spiritual guidance.

Affirmation: I'm ready to make peace with the past.

WORDS

August 11

The Eskimo have fifty-two names for snow because it is important to them; there ought to be as many for love.
—*Margaret Atwood*

Did you ever see the movie *Manhattan*? A young girl, played by Mariel Hemingway, asks, "Do you love me?" The character played by Woody Allen replies, "Do I love you? I *luv* you! I *looove* you! I *lurrve* you!"

Sometimes the word *love* falls dismally short of the intensity in our heart. Then we need to become poets, finding new, imaginative ways to express the magnitude of our affection.

My personal favorite by a recent flame was, "I'm flabbergasted by you." I really liked that.

Affirmation: Let me tell you in my own way.

Fond as we are of our loved ones, there comes at times during their absence an unexplainable peace.
　　　　　—Anne Shaw

It's great to have the bed to ourselves. To spread out, piling magazines and stationery on his side, eating ice cream, dropping cookie crumbs, and watching whatever we feel like on TV.

Brief separations, whether for business trips, a visit home, or any other reason, do wonders for romance. We can relax for a few days and enjoy our own rhythm without worrying about anyone else's needs, then reunite, excited to be together again.

Affirmation: Being alone makes me appreciate you more.

COMMITMENT

August 13

The moment one definitely commits oneself, then Providence moves too.
                                    —*Rainer Maria Rilke*

Commitment is a paradox: when we throw ourselves wholeheartedly into our relationship, we both limit and liberate ourselves.

On the surface commitment appears to put parameters around our freedom. We say, "I pledge to be exclusively with this person," which, in effect, precludes other possibilities.

In return we are freed to explore our potential fully in the safety of the secure and loving haven we've created.

Affirmation: I'm committed.

SCENE FROM A MARRIAGE: You're at a party. Out of the corner of your eye you see him watching her. She's a redhead with legs that don't quit. She is a violinist. You're wearing the same navy dress you've worn dozens of times before. You fantasize them staring into each other's eyes. You fantasize them sleeping together. You're making yourself sick, and he hasn't even said a word to her.

Stop! Stop! Stop!

Your insecurity is getting the better of you.

Even if he *is* looking at her, there's a long mile between looking, lusting, and letting ourselves fall into bed with someone else.

Here's what you need to do: First, check out the room and see if there's anyone who catches *your* attention. Go ahead and look. See—there are others you find attractive, too, which is really no major threat to your marriage.

Next excuse yourself and go to the bathroom. Look in the mirror. See how beautiful you are. Freshen your makeup and repeat the following words to yourself:

Affirmation: There are lots of beautiful people in the world. I'm glad you've chosen me.

MAKING UP

After winning an argument with his wife, the wisest thing a man can do is to apologize.

—*Anonymous*

This is good advice for both men and women. Because being the "winner" affords us the luxury of apologizing.

For what?

For being so bent on victory even at the expense of our loved one. For whatever hurt our partner has sustained in the process of our convincing them they were wrong.

An apology is a way of saying to our mate, "I'm sorry we argued. You mean more to me than winning."

Affirmation: Let's make up.

If wishes were beggars, horses would ride.
—*Newberg Abry*

This seemingly absurd saying says a lot: Simply wishing for what we want keeps us beggars instead of royalty, hoping for handouts rather than making the most of what's at hand.

The alternative is to focus on taking real, substantive steps to bring out the best in our marriage. We can sit around wishing and hoping for things to materialize, or we can take action.

Begin now. Think of three concrete ways you can enhance your relationship with your mate.

Affirmation: I will _____.
I will _____.
I will _____.

ATTITUDE

August 17

The only thing that changed was my mind.
—Laurie Nedville

One minute we think he's the greatest, the next we can't stand him.

All that's changed is how *we* look at him.

Attitude is everything. When we're positively inclined toward our mate, we can applaud his strengths and accept his limitations.

When we're angry or disappointed, we have little or no support to offer. We take his gifts for granted; his weaknesses seem incredibly annoying.

Taking on a positive outlook *doesn't* mean we ignore what's difficult, it simply means we put it in a bigger, brighter perspective.

Affirmation: I can change the way I look at him.

There are six requisites in every happy marriage. The first is faith and the remaining five are confidence.
—*Elbert Hubbard*

It takes a leap of faith to make a life commitment to another human being.

Once we are off the ground, we must summon considerable confidence: confidence that we've done the right thing; confidence that we have the guts, stamina and staying power; confidence that we can live up to our vows.

We do this by doing it. Each day we leap again, with faith in our commitment and confidence in ourselves.

Affirmation: I'm confident that I have what it takes to create a successful marriage.

FAMILY

August 19

With all beings and all things we shall be as relatives.
—Sioux Indian

Being married means being related to each other, linked as family as well as lovers and friends.

Relatives—at their best—provide support and nurturance. We can turn to them at any time and know they will be there no matter what. We would do the same.

Whether or not we become parents, marriage vows make us a family.

Affirmation: Welcome to my family.

Only free men can negotiate. Prisoners cannot enter into contracts.

—*Nelson Mandela*

We enter into the covenant of marriage freely, knowing what we're doing and doing it because we want to.

Yet sometimes we feel resentful. Trapped. Our mate expects things from us we can't deliver. We don't know how to give without giving too much of ourselves away.

At these times it's best to sit down together and talk. Talk about how to ease the pressure. Talk about ways to accommodate each other without compromising ourselves.

Contracts can continually be renegotiated based on what we are genuinely prepared to give at any given moment.

Affirmation: I'm here because I've made a conscious choice.

FUN

August 21

Are we having fun yet?
                        —Ziggy

Do you remember being a teenager and fantasizing about falling in love and getting married?

My fantasy was of an adult slumber party—laughing and cuddling and eating potato chips in bed with my best friend/lover/husband.

I *didn't,* however, fantasize about paying bills, folding laundry, or washing a sinkful of dirty dishes at ten P.M. after working all day.

Marriage is both. Sometimes it's both at once. Laughing and cuddling and eating potato chips with a pile of bills spread all over the bed.

Affirmation: It's more fun to do it together.

When change is necessary, there are two mistakes to avoid: One lies in excessive haste . . . the other lies in excessive hesitation.
—*I Ching*

Sometimes we need to make changes: big changes (a career crisis that involves a major move to another city, deciding whether or not to have a baby), smaller changes (whether to join a health club or save for a much-needed vacation).

Big or small, making sound decisions together requires clear thinking and cooperation. We need to take both partners' feelings into consideration. We need to weigh all our options carefully without getting bogged down in fear or ambivalence.

If we act prematurely, we risk jumping in the wrong direction. If we wait too long, we risk losing wonderful opportunities that can enrich our lives.

Affirmation: There's a time to leap and a time to linger over important decisions.

BABY TALK

August 23

SCENE FROM A MARRIAGE: Should you or shouldn't you? Have a baby, that is. He's ready. You're not so sure. You just turned thirty. But what about your career? This isn't the time to rock the boat, especially after the promotion you just got. What about all those adventures you promised each other (camping in the Rockies), the dream house you're saving for? You do want children. But right now?

Wait. Is there a deadline here?

Give yourself whatever reasonable extensions you need to think about and talk about all the repercussions of having a child.

Bringing a baby into the world—and into your marriage—is a huge decision. The good news is, You both know that you want to be parents. The other good news is, Time is on your side.

Take time to consider the pros and cons. Maybe with the help of a counselor who can help explore what it will mean to add a child to the equation.

Meanwhile make some of those dreams come true. Right now you have all the freedom in the world.

Affirmation: We'll have our children for the rest of our lives. There's no rush.

ANNALS OF THE WOMEN'S MOVEMENT:
I bring home the bacon and he cooks it (rarely to my satisfaction)
but who likes bacon rare?
    —*Jack Ziegler cartoon*

The trick to sharing a home-cooked meal has two parts.
Part one: Someone cooks and serves. Part two: The other
person is openly appreciative.

 This means that if he's cooking, let him do it *his* way.
This doesn't mean you have to relish raw bacon. It does
mean that you don't get to criticize or stand over him
telling him *why* to cook the bacon or *how* to cook the
bacon (suggest he buy microwave bacon—it takes four
minutes and it's great!).

 If either of you has to choke on compliments consis-
tently, there are options. Maybe one cooks and the other
takes permanent dish detail. Maybe sign up for a couples'
cooking class. Maybe order pizza.

**Affirmation: We won't let cooking spoil the
broth.**

COMMITMENT

August 25

You cannot demand complete proof before you begin something. In some things you must have blind faith.
    —Deng Ming Dao

There are no guarantees. We must enter into marriage with the willingness to give it our all, even when we're not absolutely sure. Otherwise we sit on the fence, waiting for dividends before we fully invest ourselves.

Waiting to know we're happy before we totally commit is like waiting to eat dinner until we're sure we'll be full when we're finished. We have to suspend our disbelief and simply dig into our relationship, digging in with gusto, willing to try and taste new things.

Affirmation: I'm ready to dig in.

The ability to be friends with a woman, particularly the woman you love, is to me the greatest achievement.
—Henry Miller

This is an unexpected quote from a writer long noted for wanton womanizing.

Of course he said this in his eighties, when perhaps he had come to the realization that friendship, ultimately, is as thrilling as sexual conquest.

Let's hope it doesn't take us eighty years to discover the importance of nurturing friendship between ourselves and our mate. If you aren't sure how to start, talk to a close friend and ask what it is that you give her or him. Then apply some of the same gifts to your marriage.

Affirmation: Friendship is the foundation of our love.

> *This hour I tell things in confidence,*
> *I might not tell everybody,*
> *but I tell you.*
> > —*Walt Whitman*

It's great to be confidantes. To share our most private, innermost feelings and experiences: when we were nine years old and felt horribly homesick at camp; what it was like to lose our virginity; the hopes and dreams we hold on to when we're all alone.

One of the best reasons to *not* have an extramarital affair is to protect this part of our relationship. To avoid building a wall of secrecy that eats away trust and destroys our ability to confide in one another.

This is a sacred aspect of marriage to be preserved at all costs. We must be able to tell our mate anything and everything, knowing we have nothing—*nothing*—to hide.

Affirmation: I have no secrets.

And then I asked him with my eyes to ask again yes
and then he asked me would I yes . . .
and his heart was going like mad
and yes I said yes I will Yes.
                    —James Joyce

Moments of ecstasy.

Hearts pounding, we embrace our beloved, surrendering to the sweet, sweet magic of making love with the one whose eyes and lips say yes to us again and again.

We can take turns asking and responding. Saying yes to the continuous awakening of our passion for one another.

Affirmation: Yes!

August 29

If everyone sweeps in front of his own door, the whole city will be clean.

—*Anonymous*

Sometimes we act like an army recruiter, overly invested in getting our partner to improve. We nudge him and drill him to be All That He Can Be (Read: all that *we* want him to be). We're the resident expert on his shortcomings. If only he'd ask! We know *just* what he needs in order to be happier and more fulfilled!

Despite our best intentions, running a boot camp for his personal growth is a way to avoid looking honestly at ourselves. We need to clean up our act and trust that he'll clean up his own.

Affirmation: I'll focus on ways to improve myself and trust he'll do the same.

I am alone with the beating of my heart.
—Lui Chi

Sometimes we feel alone even in our marriage. We feel isolated, lost, unable to find common ground.

We needn't feel afraid. Just because we're not feeling close doesn't mean our relationship is disintegrating; we're simply in a phase of healthy separateness, which can be a sweet time to enjoy our own company or a critical time to pursue our own growth.

Knowing we can move apart and come back together —relishing our solitude as well as our sharing—is one mark of a successful marriage.

Affirmation: I am comfortable with my solitude as well as with the moments when our hearts beat as one.

ABUNDANCE

August 31

We learn the magical lesson that making the most of what we have turns it into more.
> —Melody Beattie

There's much to be said for the "half full" school of looking at things.

We can easily forget to appreciate what's wonderful about our mate: He's chronically late. But on the other hand he's affectionate, has a great sense of humor, and knows how to fix things! She constantly forgets where her keys are, *but* she's sensitive, stimulating, and the best Trivial Pursuit player in the world.

As autumn draws near, let us stop and take stock of all we have. It's usually more than we think.

Affirmation: My life is more than half full.

Of all men, Adam was the happiest; he had no mother-in-law.
—François Parfaict

Dealing with extended family—including mothers-in-law—can be stressful, satisfying, or both. After all, we share holidays and life passages, spending an awful lot of time with people we never chose as friends.

If we're comfortable and compatible, great! If not, we still need to make the effort to get to know—and get along with—our in-laws and other members of our new extended family.

This is an effort worth making. As my own mother always said, "You don't just marry a person; you marry their entire family."

As you approach Labor Day, whether or not you're spending the holiday with them, make a commitment to yourself to find common ground. If nothing else, you love the same person. That's a start.

Affirmation: I'm willing to extend myself.

September 2

God gave burdens, also shoulders.
              —*Yiddish saying*

Shoulders to cry on, shoulders to lean on when we feel overwhelmed by the demands of day-to-day life.

We need to be able to turn to each other. This doesn't mean we are needy or dependent; one of the "perks" of marriage is that we can count on our mate to lessen our load without fear of judgment or rejection.

We can hold each other up, taking turns being strong or shaky, sharing the burdens by offering solace and a shoulder.

Affirmation: I'm here for you whenever you need me.

Some people pay a compliment as if they expect a receipt.
—Kim Hubbard

It's not that we're keeping score exactly, we just want acknowledgment for having noticed something we appreciate about our mate and saying so!

But being nice is its own reward. If not, it's a setup. When we count our compliments and wait for them to be paid back, we put unfair pressure on our mate and diminish the pleasure of giving.

The best compliments are spontaneous and free. I see you. I like you. I tell you. Period.

Affirmation: My compliments are free of charge.

FIXING HER

September 4

SCENE FROM A MARRIAGE: *She's been down for almost a week, moping around the house, eating chocolate—and little else—dragging in from work and falling asleep in front of the TV. You keep trying to talk to her, but she just sighs. Or yells at you to leave her alone. You're getting worried. And frustrated. Can't she do something to snap out of it?*

Obviously not. And all your nagging won't help.

This is one of the hardest parts of marriage—to sit by patiently, genuinely concerned, instead of trying to "fix" our mate.

Right now she doesn't need anyone talking her out of her feelings, telling her to get better and *hurry up about it!*

Your job is to wait and watch. This may be a temporary slump, in which case she needs acceptance and understanding. If, however, she continues to be depressed, urge her to get help. Offer to go with her, and make sure she knows that you love her no matter what.

Affirmation: I can support you, but I can't fix you.

Where two are gathered, there is home.
　　　　　　　—Sally Gerheart

Home is how we *feel* when we are together. It is knowing we are safe to be totally ourselves, without apology. It is the warm comfort of walking down the street hand-in-hand, then coming back at the end of the day, laughing, commiserating, supporting each other for what it takes to be out in the world.

Home is where we return, where we let down, find solace, and know we are secure.

Affirmation: With you I am at home.

OLD FLAMES

September 6

Being divorced is like being hit by a Mack truck. If you live through it, you start looking very carefully to the left and the right.

—Deborah Kerr

Those of us who have survived divorce or other serious breakups and chosen to remarry are a little black-and-blue. We tread carefully, looking for the pitfalls, looking to avoid a repeat performance of the pain we've been dealt in the past.

We can—and should—learn from experience. Hopefully we're wiser; we know what worked, what didn't, and how to avoid reenacting destructive patterns.

It's natural to be cautious, but we must be willing to start over. Really start over. With a clean slate and an optimistic attitude.

We must also be willing to move forward, investing heart and soul, believing this is truly forever.

Affirmation: I will make the most of my experience.

As a friend of mine told her horrified mother, "He didn't adopt me, he married me."
— Anna Quindlen

Changing our names when we marry—which used to be a given—can now be a complicated dilemma. Some of us assume we will take on our husband's name. Some of us are appalled at this antiquated idea, and others of us are totally confused about what's right to do.

What's right to do is whatever is right for both of you. This is a serious decision. You will have to be very honest about your feelings, considering questions such as, How strongly do each of you feel about your position? Why? What repercussions will your choices have down the road?

Remember, there are lots of options—your name, his name, hyphenated names, even a brand-new name. You can take your time on this (some couples decide a year or two down the road) and do anything you want, as long as you can both live with it.

Affirmation: Together we will find what works for us.

RIVALRY

I don't think you can have a happy marriage if you're continually elbowing your husband and jockeying for position.
—Danielle Steel

And you can't have a happy marriage if you're continually elbowing your *wife* and jockeying for position.

This works both ways! Rivalry is natural between mates: you get a raise, and he's still scrambling; his friends seem eager to get to know you, while yours seem cool and standoffish toward him. When we compare ourselves with the person closest to us, we may resent their accomplishment and withhold our support.

We need to shift from competitiveness to cooperation. If we can stop one-upping and boost each other, we both stand to gain.

**Affirmation: I am happy for your successes.
Please be happy for mine.**

SCENE FROM A MARRIAGE: It's taken eight months to drag him here. Now he's here, but he hasn't said a word. He sits staring off into space, apparently somewhere between bored and disgusted. Why isn't the counselor making him talk?!? Why are you here? Is this an exercise in futility?

No. There *is* hope, but you need realistic expectations, which can only exist if you have the right information to base them on.

Here's what you need to know:

First, decide what *you* want to get out of counseling (and how you will measure results) not how you want *him* to change!

Second, you need to commit to a time frame that you can live with.

Now you can go forward knowing what you want and how long you're willing to wait. And remember, it's okay for him to be ambivalent. He's there, and that's plenty for now.

Affirmation: Rome wasn't built in a day.

ABANDON

Spend it all. Shout it, play it, love it, all, right now, every time!
—Annie Dillard

We must live the days of our marriage as if they were our last. Making sure to hold each other close in our heart each and every morning before we part. Saying "I love you" often, especially when it's least expected. Telling each other all the things we appreciate and how much life is enhanced from being together.

Every time we have the opportunity, we must seize it and show our affection. Real love is not to be squandered.

Affirmation: I give you my all.

Most people would rather get than give affection.
—*Aristotle*

I don't know about that.

Have you ever watched people at a birthday party? The gift givers often seem more excited than the person tearing open the wrapping.

It feels great to give! There is tremendous pleasure and satisfaction in it, whether it's calling to find out if there's anything we can pick up on the way home or wrapping our arms around our sweetheart when he needs a hug.

Maybe there's no real way to separate giving and getting. When love moves us to show affection, this is joy itself.

Affirmation: Loving you is at least as satisfying as being loved by you.

INTOLERANCE

September 12

If you hate a person, you hate something in him that is part of yourself.
>—Hermann Hesse

The things that drive us to distraction about our mate are often shadows of the very things we struggle with in ourselves. His wishy-washiness brings up all the times we wish we hadn't been so passive. Her angry outbursts are frightening reminders of the moments we've lost control.

It's hard to be tolerant of our mate's flaws when they echo our own. We can't expect ourselves to be perfectly objective—and supportive—at all times. We *can* ask ourselves to be honest when something hits close to home. To say, "I'm willing to look at this so that I can better accept you . . . and myself."

Affirmation: My intolerance is a mirror of my own lack of self-acceptance.

SCENE FROM A MARRIAGE: BZZZZZZZZZ!!!! *The alarm goes off, shattering your blissful sleep. It's five-thirty. He's got a seven A.M. plane. You don't have to be up until eight. He reaches over and hits the snooze button . . . you drift back to sleep . . .* BZZZZZZZZZ!!! *He hits it again. . . . If that damn thing goes off one more time . . .*

You may hit *him!*

Okay, don't hit him, but you're right to be angry. When we live together, we need to respect each other's schedules, especially each other's sleep. We're too busy, too hassled, to lose one minute of precious rest.

This is a fairly black-and-white situation. You're right. He's wrong. But try to hold your temper. Screaming at him will only wake you up more.

Option 1: If you can, calmly ask him to turn off the alarm and get going so that you can get back to sleep. If you're too mad to be civil, don't say anything. Wait until later, then ask him to be more considerate in the future.

Option 2: Get up with him, make coffee, and give him a loving send-off. Then head back to bed.

Affirmation: Let's start over.

RECIPROCITY

September 14

Most marriages are run like a commodities market, with loving behaviors the coin in trade.
—Harville Hendrix

Marriage is, in some ways, an arrangement of exchanges: He pays the bills while you work out for an hour; you brave the crowds to do Christmas shopping while he goes cross-country skiing.

Reciprocity is fine, as long as love isn't the currency.

When we begin to trade love for sex or security or financial support, we cheapen our relationship. Our love mustn't have a price tag. We can—and should—help each other; equitably, often, and without keeping tabs.

Affirmation: What can I do for you?

The summer night you strolled up . . . dressed in a white linen suit and carrying lilacs you'd lifted from your mother's yard . . . I knew that all was lost for love.
— Larkin Warren

Close your eyes and remember the very first time you laid eyes on him, the first time he reached for your hand . . . your lips . . . the first moment you knew you wanted to marry him.

These memories are locked like timeless treasures within the safe-deposit box of our hearts. We can retrieve them at will, for sheer pleasure or for those periods when looking back gives us the confidence to look ahead.

Affirmation: I remember.

CHANGE

September 16

When you are through changing, you are through.
    —*Bruce Bartons*

In her book, *Staying Married in the Age of Divorce,* author Fran Klansburg says the ability to withstand change is the mark of a successful relationship.

So much changes over the years: apartments, houses, babies, careers, friendships that come and go. Changes inevitably create stress and anxiety, as well as great opportunities for growth.

Changes bring on times of trial or times of triumph depending on how flexible we are. Hopefully we remain close throughout the passages. Hopefully they strengthen our love.

Affirmation: I'm flexible.

For you and I are past our dancing days.
—from Romeo and Juliet, *by William Shakespeare*

These ill-fated lovers never got their honeymoon.

But for most of us there is no such abrupt time limit to how long we can go on dancing.

As we settle into married life, we may trade our black patent high heels for tennis shoes; romantic nights in smoky cabarets for popcorn in front of the television.

Hanging out comfortably at home is great, but it's just as important to make time for real dates. Dinner out, necking in a darkened movie theater, slow-dancing together late into the night, help us to stay lovers always.

Affirmation: Let's dance.

SEX

September 18

Sex: The most fun you can have without laughing.
                                    —*Anonymous*

Which is one reason why it's so important to make time for making love.

Although personally I prefer the sort of sex that makes you laugh. Or cry. Or both at the same time.

As we ripen in each other's commitment, we are more able to let go, to let lovemaking be spontaneous, whatever it is at any given moment—sometimes a ton of fun, sometimes burning and passionate, sometimes a way of releasing tension and falling happily asleep in each other's arms.

Affirmation: I'm open to all sorts of lovemaking.

Make yourself necessary to someone.
　　　　　—*Ralph Waldo Emerson*

We start with our mate, making time to listen, making every effort to be a helpmate, making life easier for each other however we can.

However, we mustn't confuse caring and caretaking—interdependency and indispensability. Interdependency involves give-and-take; indispensability involves taking over at the expense of our mate's independence and autonomy.

We must be necessary to each other's lives, without rescuing, saving, or doing for our partners what they can do for themselves.

Affirmation: I'm here to support you as long as you can stand on your own two feet.

GRATITUDE

September 20

The sum which two married people owe to one another defies calculation . . . which can only be discharged through all eternity.

—*Johann Wolfgang von Goethe*

We owe each other everything and nothing; infinite gratitude for countless gifts of love, yet nothing at all. For how can we possibly repay what we've been given?

Perhaps over time we repay not only each other but the world as well. With acts of creativity: the home we build together, the work we complete with each other's encouragement, the children we nurture who carry our legacy into the future.

We settle our debt by taking the love that's given and redistributing it, wherever and however we can.

Affirmation: I am forever grateful for how you've changed my life.

> *Share everything.*
> *Play fair.*
> *Flush.*
> —Robert Fulghum

These three items from best-selling author Robert Fulghum's list of what we learned in kindergarten is easily adapted for marriage. Especially the third one.

Flushing or not and leaving the toilet seat up or down are just the sorts of things couples fight about. Superficial concerns? Refer to items 1 and 2.

1. *Share everything.* It's important to respect each other's sensibilities—environmentally (why waste water by flushing every time?) and aesthetically ("I can't stand it when you leave toilet paper in the toilet!").

2. *Play fair.* Have you ever fallen into the toilet in the middle of the night, sleepily assuming the seat was down when it was up?

Little things become big things unless we work them out.

Affirmation: I will also pay attention to the seemingly insignificant issues.

POSSESSIVENESS

September 22

We would bristle at "cave man" possessiveness, but wish he wasn't completely blasé when we're off to a sales conference with forty-two men.
> —Ellen Sue Stern

Everyone envied Pamela. John sent her flowers at work, showered her with affection, went everywhere with her.

It was *so* romantic! Until she went to a work party and he showed up drunk and picked a fight with her new boss, who he insisted was flirting with her!

There's a limit. We want him to be a little possessive; this "I'm fine with whatever you do" attitude makes us worry he's not the least bit concerned. Still, we don't want to be strangled by his grip.

Here's my fantasy: We're at a party. A good-looking man approaches me. My husband puts his arm around me, kisses me on the mouth, then walks away.

Affirmation: I belong to myself. I choose to be with you.

SCENE FROM A MARRIAGE: For the third time this week she has her secretary call to say she's working late and won't be home until nine. This executive stuff is great, but what about your marriage? Besides, she's killing herself! She hasn't had a proper dinner in days, and it's been weeks since you spent a night together without her briefcase by the bed. You know her career is important, but is this how life is going to be?

Let's hope not.

With all our pressures—economic and otherwise—it's easy to get trapped into working ourselves to death.

It can also be the death of our marriage if we're not careful. Relationships need to be nurtured, with time and attention, especially relaxed time when we're not distracted by thoughts of business calls and the endless pile of work on our desk.

If this is situational—seasonal pressures or an unexpected visit from the New York brass—then by all means give her some slack. If not, tell her you understand how important her work is, but that you're concerned about her all-consuming schedule. Ask if there's any way you can help. And be sure to say how much you miss her.

Affirmation: I promise not to let my work take precedence over our relationship.

LIBERATION

September 24

You might say that the entire male sex has come out of the closet in the late twentieth century; real men do wear scent, read Iris Murdoch and eat escargot.
　　　　　　　　　　　　—Anne Rice

Some "real men" wouldn't be caught dead buying goat cheese, and that's all right too!

What's important is freedom of choice. The freedom to dress however he feels comfortable—whether it's jeans and T-shirts or a suit and tie. Freedom to have *Esquire* and *Cosmo* on either side of the bed. Freedom to eat escargot, pot roast, and potatoes, or anything in-between.

Life gets better as we break out of the bonds of gender-identified behavior, as "real men," just like "real women," become freer and freer to express themselves as whole human beings.

Affirmation: I like the "real" you.

Magic is the art of turning negatives into positives, of spinning straw into gold.

—Starhawk

Marriage is a natural setting in which to work such magic: It presents us with the crisis that ultimately brings us closer to each other, the sickness that serves as a catalyst for recommitting to the values we share.

Often we aren't aware of the potential for transformation until after the fact; we look back and recognize the seeds of blessing planted in times of adversity.

We can learn to identify these golden opportunities as they arise—by knowing there is a positive, hopeful side of what's before us, by turning to each other and saying:

Affirmation: Together we will face this, and together we will be blessed.

TOLERANCE

September 26

What I cannot love, I overlook.
                    —Anaïs Nin

If I had one goal in marriage, this would be it: to be able to overlook, even to embrace, those qualities in my partner that make me cringe. To love him in spite of his flaws, knowing it is I who needs to learn to be more tolerant rather than *he* who needs to change.

Overlooking doesn't mean we lower our standards for our mate; it means we raise our standards of ourselves.

Affirmation: I will look for the best in my partner and accept the rest.

Constant togetherness is fine—but only for Siamese twins.
—Victoria Billings

There are marriages where couples stick together like glue, doing everything and going everywhere together, and other marriages where partners are highly independent.

Both work. It's a question of balance.

If we only have each other, we don't have enough in our lives. We need to widen our circles, involving ourselves in separate activities and friendships that satisfy us individually.

But we can also lose sight of each other if the circle becomes too large. Our relationship comes first, everything else follows.

Affirmation: Let's stick together without sticking to each other.

PROTECTIVENESS

September 28

One of the oldest human needs is having someone to wonder where you are when you don't come home at night.
—Margaret Mead

We spend our teenage years screaming at our parents, "Don't wait up for me," then wish someone would do so when we're long past the age of answering to anyone.

Being worried about is one way we feel loved. We want to be accounted for, our presence noted, our absence missed.

Even if it's just crawling into bed and having him roll over and murmur, "Honey, you're home." That's enough.

Affirmation: I'm glad you worry about me.

I was at a party feeling very shy. . . . A beautiful young man offered me some salted peanuts, and as he as handed them to me, he said, "I wish they were emeralds," and that was the end of my heart.

—Helen Hayes

Gestures—whether simple or grand—go a long way toward making us feel loved.

We needn't get emeralds to feel like royalty. In fact sometimes the little things say more—a handful of daisies on a blustery February afternoon; the tape of our favorite music he painstakingly puts together; remembering to pick up his favorite chocolate drop cookies just to please him.

Thoughtful gestures are a way of saying, "I'm thinking of you and searched out a way to say how special you are to me."

Affirmation: It's the little things.

VULNERABILITY

If you don't share [trouble] you don't give the person who loves you enough chance to love you enough.
          —Dinah Shore

Trouble is meant to be shared.

When we act invulnerable, as if "I can handle everything on my own, thank you very much," we deny our mate one of the greatest privileges of marriage; getting to be there for each other.

This is part of loving another person—to be privy to inner struggles. To problem-solve, to show up with Kleenex and soup when we're battling the flu, to hold each other when we've got the blues.

We need to give each other this chance. Otherwise we don't let love do its work.

Affirmation: I'm ready to let you in.

If he sins against you seven times a day, and returns to you seven times, saying "I repent," forgive him.
—Luke 17:14

C'mon!

There's a point at which saying "I'm sorry" is just another way of avoiding a scene.

Apologies are a big first step. But if they only serve to purge ourselves, they bring temporary relief and buy time. Which is no guarantee anything will change. In fact the more often we hear repentence without any tangible new behavior, the more likely we are to feel ourselves subjected to a scam.

Forgiveness is right and fine, but only as long as it's accompanied by a plan of action and a commitment to follow through.

Affirmation: I will show you that I am serious about making changes.

COMPATIBILITY

October 2

Ever since I can remember, I've longed for a soul mate.
—Linda Schierse Leonard

Soul mate: Someone who understands us intuitively without our uttering a single word. Someone whose values, dreams, and spirit match our own.

Our spouse may or may not be our soul mate. Some of us marry our mirror image; our relationship flows easily and naturally, with few rough edges.

Others of us have to struggle for common ground with our mates. Our relationship thrives on friction and a different sort of energy than a "soul-mate connection."

What we long for in a life partner is unique to each of us. When we find it, it brings gladness to our hearts.

Affirmation: We can be heart mates without being soul mates.

Love is what happens to men and women who don't know each other.

—*W. Somerset Maugham*

This quote rankles me.

I don't like the idea that once we get beneath the surface, love wears off.

Just the opposite is true. Love deepens as we really come to know each other. As our facade falls away, we trade illusion for intimacy; disillusionment—the stripping away of illusions—makes way for a stronger, more sustaining love, based on seeing each other as we really are.

Affirmation: I have no illusions.

"WAS IT GOOD FOR YOU?"

October 4

> SCENE FROM A MARRIAGE: *You're feeling inse-*
> *cure. It seemed like he liked it, but now you're not sure.*
> *There was that moment when he grabbed you and called out*
> *your name . . . but . . . well . . . how are you sup-*
> *posed to know whether it was everything he wanted?*

Ask.

Sometimes it's awkward, especially when silence follows lovemaking.

But the only way to know whether our partner is truly satisfied is to take the risk and find out. If you're afraid to break the silence, afraid you'll appear silly or stupid, remember: if you're intimate enough with each other to take your clothes off, you're intimate enough to talk about what happens when you do.

You don't have to be blatant. Try "How're you doing?" or "What would make you feel good?" The answers will begin to tell you what you need to know.

Affirmation: I want to please you.

The pain of loving you is almost more than I can bear.
   —D. H. Lawrence

Sometimes love tears us open. It hurts because we care so deeply. Because we've invested our all and know how much we stand to lose.

The pain of loving also comes at times when we don't feel intimate. When we hurt each other, intentionally or inadvertently, when we're separated or simply aren't feeling close.

Love makes us raw to a world of feelings; there is a price to pay for being so alive, and we pay it with both our pain and our pleasure.

Affirmation: I can bear it.

EXPECTATIONS

October 6

Blessed be he who expects nothing, for he shall never be disappointed.
—Alexander Pope

Talk about hedging your bet!

I'd rather advocate throwing caution to the wind and ourselves fully into our relationships.

True, keeping expectations in check and leaning on the side of safety reduces our risk of getting hurt. It also lessens the chances of experiencing ecstasy.

Life is too short! If we don't expect anything, that's what we'll get. If we expect a lot, we may get more than we're hoping for.

Affirmation: I'll take my chances.

Always there remains portions of the heart unto which no one is able to enter, invite them as we may.
—Mary Dixon Thayer

Close as we are, each of us remains an individual with private recesses known only to ourselves.

As we become more intimate, we also learn to respect each other's privacy. We explore where we are welcome and discover what is off-limits. We sense—or are told—when our mate is ready to share and when loving him means leaving him alone with his thoughts.

Protecting the secret places of the heart is an inalienable marital right. In doing so, we discover that we can be separate and united, that we can love another person without losing ourselves.

Affirmation: I reserve the right to remain private.

October 8

What greater thing is there for two human souls than to find that they are joined for life.
—*George Eliot*

We are not just any two people, thrown together like random college roommates, figuring out how to share bathroom space, negotiate schedules, and tiptoe around each other's moods.

Knowing we are two souls who are meant to be together, whose essences are joined for eternity, helps us to get through the everyday struggles of mortal coexistence. Knowing we have found each other for a reason—even if that reason is beyond our full comprehension—keeps us committed to a sacramental marriage: a lifelong partnership of caring, learning, and devotion.

Affirmation: Our love is destined.

Wife: a former sweetheart.
> —*H. L. Mencken*

It's a shame if we stop courting each other when we say "I do."

That's exactly when we need to redouble our efforts at romance—using terms of endearment, showing up unexpectedly with flowers, embracing in public just because we just can't keep our hands off each other.

We should never feel we've sacrificed our "sweetheart" status for that of spouse. Being husband and wife means being sweethearts for life.

Affirmation: Let me call you sweetheart.

MASTURBATION

October 10

Don't knock masturbation—it's sex with someone I love.
—Woody Allen

Being married implies sexual fidelity—with one exception.

We still continue to have a sexual relationship with ourselves. It's perfectly fine to give ourselves pleasure at times when we need a release, when our partner is unavailable, or when we're simply tuned in alone to our sexuality. We may want to do so privately, make masturbation part of our repertoire with our mate, or use it to complement our marital sex life.

This is nothing to be ashamed of. Knowing what we like—and how to give ourselves what we need—is part of being a vital, healthy, responsible adult.

Affirmation: I always have me.

All that we send into the lives of others comes back into our own.
—*Edwin Markham*

We reap the benefits of all the ways we support our mate. Our unwavering belief in her gives her confidence to go after the job of a lifetime; his physical tenderness helps heal our insecurities, freeing us to feel better about ourselves.

What we get is not always immediately apparent; it may seem as if we're giving and giving without getting back. But every single thing we do to strengthen our spouse inevitably serves to strengthen our marriage. The more each of us has, the more each of us has to give.

Affirmation: Whatever I give comes back to me.

SEXISM

October 12

I can bring home the bacon, fry it up in a pan. And never, never, never let you forget you're a man.
—1978 ad for Enjoli perfume

Amazing how much has changed in a mere fifteen years! Today this same ad would be grist for a *Saturday Night Live* routine satirizing sexist notions of what women are supposed to do to shore up "their man's" ego.

Today we each bring home the bacon; we each know how to fry it (and if we don't, it's time to learn!). Neither of us needs to diminish our achievements or earning power to protect the other.

Thank goodness we've learned that being a man *and* being a woman means being able to bring home the bacon, fry it, and take turns serving it to each other.

Affirmation: I don't have to massage your ego to express my love.

SCENE FROM A MARRIAGE: You're settling in. The honeymoon's over, you've returned three toaster ovens, written dozens of thank-you notes, and now . . . well, now what? Every day is pretty much the same—work, dinner, bills, an occasional movie out with friends. You look at him across the kitchen table, and a horrifying thought enters your mind: Is this all there is?

Yes. This is it.

And while this may strike you as a terrible disappointment, the truth is that marriage is both less *and* more than the love songs say.

It's a letdown to drop back to earth after all the planning, waiting, and anticipation. We're left with the reality of everyday life; we still have all the same routines, pressures, and responsibilities we had before.

On the other hand we get to share them with another person. The satisfaction of sitting across the kitchen table, over weeks, months, and years, slowly absorbing the most intimate details of another human being's life transports and satisfies us long after the honeymoon is over.

Affirmation: This is just the beginning.

SELF-DISCOVERY

October 14

I didn't discover Barbara Walters; she discovered herself.
—Hugh Downs

Although Hugh Downs was Barbara Walters's mentor, not her husband, the same could be said of many spouses.

We don't discover each other so much as we help each other to discover ourselves. We see ourselves in a new light through the eyes of our beloved. He marvels at our sensual lips; we check them out in the mirror. We admire his grace under pressure; he begins to pride himself on it.

As we unfold through our partner's perceptions, we gain a fresh—often better—look at ourselves.

Affirmation: You help me look at myself differently.

You cannot teach a man anything. You can only help him to find it within himself.
　　　　　　—Galileo Galilei

It's hard to live with another person day after day without wanting to correct him or her. If we're not careful, we treat each other like projects perpetually in need of a finishing touch.

But we're all so sensitive to others' designs on us. Even when it comes from love, we feel defensive about our mate telling us what to do and how to do it.

Instead we can gently encourage each other to find what we need within ourselves by in effect saying, "I see how wonderful you are and how much you are capable of!"

Affirmation: My mate deserves gentle encouragement.

SPIRIT

October 16

We must remove the word impossible from our vocabulary.
—Bernie S. Siegel, M.D.

In *Love, Medicine & Miracles* Dr. Bernie Siegel shares his close-up views of a lot of suffering *and* a lot of healing.

He illuminates what the human spirit is capable of when we put our mind in a positive frame.

Whether it's fighting cancer or making important changes in our marriage, the word *impossible* is our enemy. It locks out hope. It keeps us from putting forth our most valiant effort. It keeps us from being able to envision what *is* possible if we care enough and keep believing it's worth it to try.

Affirmation: It's possible.

ADVANTAGES OF HEARTBREAK:
1. *More room in bed.*
2. *Time slows to a crawl.*
3. *Opportunity to get in touch with your weeping.*
   —from Love Is Hell, *by Matt Groening*

This cartoon from *Love Is Hell* is funny, yet it has a serious message: There's something to be gained from those times when our relationship causes us pain and heartache.

When we're sad, it's good to curl up in bed with a book or our journal or our teddy bear and reflect on what's happening inside.

Time *does* slow down when we're having troubles. We should take advantage of it to lay back, stew, and feel sorry for ourselves.

And there's nothing like a good, hard cry. Things usually look up after that.

Affirmation: My heart hurts because I feel so much.

SEX

We feel better after good sex; it puts a spring in your step, a sparkle in your eye, a glow in your skin.
  —Robert Ornstein, Ph.D., and David Sobel, M.D.

Making love on a regular basis is energizing and nurturing; it heightens our overall sense of well-being and brings us closer to each other.

It's easy to let sex take a backseat to all life's everyday demands, saving it for Saturday nights or special occasions. The less sexually active we are, the more it fades into the background. And conversely the more we make love, the more we get in touch with how great it feels to give ourselves over to being sensual, sexual, and intimate with our mate.

Affirmation: I want you to touch me.

I'm mad as hell and I'm not going to take it anymore!
—*from* Network, *by Paddy Chayefsky*

Do you ever feel like you've had it? Like one more problem and you'll throw in the towel?

No matter how much we love our mate, some things make us angry—even rageful—especially when we ask over and over again and nothing changes. We reach a point where we're just good and sick of putting up with it!

Then we need to find healthy ways to vent our anger. Sometimes yelling is effective, as long as we're not abusive, as long as we say, "I'm mad!" not "You're bad!"

Sometimes we need to pound on a pillow, go for an exhausting run, or take time out. Whatever it takes to cool down until we're ready to talk reasonably about what's bothering us.

Ultimatums are a last resort. Don't use them unless you're really at the breaking point and prepared to follow through.

Affirmation: I'm mad as hell.
                  Here's what I need: _____.

ORDINARY PLEASURES

Stirring the oatmeal is a humble act . . . it represents a will-ingness to find meaning in the simple unromantic tasks: earning a living, living within a budget, putting out the garbage.
—Robert A. Johnson

My dear friends Martha and Michael included this quote in their wedding vows. It expressed their commitment to be friends as well as lovers, to bring sacred meaning to the marriage by sharing the mundane as well as the mystical.

For the past nine months I have watched them prepare for the birth of their first child. At one point Michael spent the better part of two weeks on a ladder insulating the windows on the porch so that there wouldn't be a draft; Martha shopped for strollers and read books on breast-feeding. Together they spent hours talking about how to be good parents to their child.

Today Alexander was born. Their love for each other is his best birthday gift.

Affirmation: Our commitment is a strong foundation.

Perfect love casts out fear.
            —I John, Corinthians

Early in our relationship Joey said something to me for which I will be forever grateful. He said, "I want you to never, ever be afraid with me."

His words have reverberated many times: when we've had an argument and I've been halfway out the door; when I've felt like censoring myself instead of rocking the boat; when I've been tempted to hide some not-so-perfect part of myself for fear of his anger or disapproval.

If we have even one relationship where we never have to be afraid, we walk in the world with greater confidence and security.

Affirmation: I have nothing to be afraid of.

MOVEMENT

October 22

If you want to write, you have to be willing to be disturbed.
—Kate Green

The same is true if you want to be in love.

Being in an intimate relationship shakes our identity, our values, our entire view of the world.

Sometimes we don't want to be disturbed. We don't want to be questioned or confronted with rethinking who we are or what we're about. We'd rather stay in the "comfort zone" of our existing perspectives.

At other times the challenge is exhilarating. Our marriage is the driving force of our desire to evolve.

Here's the balance: times of calm, where we can lie back and just be; times of confrontation, where we stretch and grow.

Affirmation: I'm willing to move outside of my comfort zone.

SCENE FROM A MARRIAGE: You're having a perfectly nice dinner. Or so you thought. Okay, so maybe you're a little quiet, but you're tired. You have a lot on your mind. She fiddles with her food, sighs loudly, then turns to you and says, "What are you thinking?"

You're not thinking anything.

But *she's* thinking there's something wrong. Maybe you're mad at her. Maybe you're bored with her. Maybe, just maybe, you don't love her anymore and don't know how to break the news.

Our imaginations run wild when we don't know what's going on. Even when nothing's going on. Your withdrawal scares her; she needs to be reassured that you're simply not in the mood to talk.

Tell her, "Honey, it's nothing about you. I'm just distracted." A few short words will gentle her fears.

Affirmation: I trust that your silence isn't saying something about me.

CELEBRATION

October 24

Your intimate relationship is the most precious gift in your life. It deserves some time every day to be celebrated.
—*Barbara De Angelis*

We must never, ever take our marriage for granted. It's a labor of love—and yes, conscious effort—to devote a few moments every day to display our affection for our mate.

It doesn't take much: a shared shower in the morning, a sexy message on his answering machine at work, a little note in his lunchbox, a long hug before we turn off the lights.

These are the little-things-that-go-a-long-way. We *all* need them, no matter how secure we are in our relationship. We *all* need daily reminders that we are loved and appreciated.

Affirmation: Have I told you today how much I love you?

There is no pillow so soft as a clear conscience.
—*Anonymous*

Every marriage has secrets: the kiss we stole with an old boyfriend the night before the wedding; the thirty-five dollars we skimmed off the grocery money to buy that sweater we couldn't live without; the confidence we broke by telling our best friend about the terrible fight we promised to keep to ourselves.

Knowing which secrets to tell and which to keep depends on whether it will help or harm your relationship. Here's how to know: If secrecy will erode trust and poison the intimacy between you, then get it out in the open and get it over with. If all confessing will do is relieve your conscience while causing unnecessary heartache, keep it to yourself.

Affirmation: I will rigorously examine my motivations.

October 26

There's always room for improvement—it's the biggest room in the house.
                                        —*Louise Heath Leber*

If we're not careful, marriage can become an endless encounter group in which each partner analyzes and tells the other how to be.

None of us is perfect.

And we needn't be. We are all flawed human beings trying to do our best with what we've got.

Doing the best we can means looking honestly at *ourselves,* not taking our partner's "inventory," not making ourselves his therapist, but encountering our own weaknesses and strengths and deciding what to do with them.

Affirmation: I'll work on me.

Young. Old. Just words.
> —*George Burns*

Being married may make us feel old. Settled down. We see the next fifty years flash before our eyes and wonder what happened to our youth.

Being married can also make us feel young. Adventurous. We have the rest of our lives ahead of us, and the best is yet to come.

It's a matter of attitude. We can imagine our spouse as the thief in the night who robbed us of our youth. *Or* we can see him as a playmate and fellow adventurer, with whom we will continually discover new worlds.

Affirmation: Let's grow young together.

FIGHTING

October 28

The test of a man's or woman's breeding is how they behave in a quarrel.
——*George Bernard Shaw*

I know couples who play dirty, who in the midst of a brawl say horrible things to each other.

Other couples put a lid on it; they fight fair, only saying what's necessary, censoring hurtful words they might regret.

When the dust settles, we still have to live together. Words said in anger don't evaporate; they hang in the air, polluting our relationship. They ring in our ears, even after we apologize.

Saying, "I didn't mean it," after the fact doesn't mean much. We have to fight carefully, taking full responsibility for every word that comes out of our mouths.

Affirmation: Words can be weapons. I will be careful what I say.

Happiness can only be felt if you don't set any conditions.
—*Artur Rubenstein*

We go into marriage with preset conditions: "I'll be happy if he dries the dishes, is nice to my parents, and rubs my back without wanting sex."

But what if he never dries the dishes, barely tolerates your parents, and wants to make love every time he touches you?

We need to set aside our conditions without compromising our bottom-line needs. Ask yourself these questions: *Is it critical or is it a way of testing his love? Am I pressuring him to be someone he's not? Am I missing what is there because I'm so focused on what* isn't?

If these are critical needs, then ask him to come through, just because they matter to you. If not, you need to let go so that you can appreciate all the other ways he naturally shows his love.

Affirmation: My bottom-line needs are worth fighting for. I will let the rest go.

October 30

From each according to his abilities, to each according to his needs.

—*Karl Marx*

Communism may be dead, but this is still a sound motto for marriage.

We each give what we can and take what we need. It doesn't have to be equal; in fact it can't be. We have different talents, abilities, and contributions to make. And we need different things in order to be happy and secure.

The best marriages are complementary—you're good at fixing toilets, he's great at midnight snacks. You like to talk, he likes to listen.

It doesn't matter who's giving or taking as long as each of you gets what you need.

Affirmation: I will give what I can and take what I need.

You are not required to complete the work, but neither are you at liberty to abstain from it.

—*Rabbi Tarfon*

We will never love our mate enough. We will never be as generous or thoughtful or compassionate as we'd like to be.

That's okay. The work of marriage is an ongoing process in which we aspire to be the best partner possible, setting goals, meeting some of them, falling short in ways, and trying again.

As the days shorten and winter draws near, what's important is to recommit to be fully in our marriage. To engage in the process with all our mind, all our heart, all our soul.

Affirmation: I'll do my best.

EMOTIONAL RISK

November 1

There is no way to take the danger out of human relationships.
—Barbara Grizzuti Harrison

It is always risky to become emotionally involved with another human being. We put ourselves on the line, expose our vulnerabilities, and can't be sure our feelings will be handled with care.

Sometimes we're up to it; other times our own junk gets in the way—we're tired or anxious or too pressured to give our mate the attention he needs and deserves.

Then we need to go the extra mile. This is what it means to be married—to extend our limits and tap the sources of energy and love required to be there for one another.

Affirmation: You're worth the risk.

Occupation is essential.
—*Virginia Woolf*

The more we develop ourselves, the more we bring to our relationship. Finding our calling, doing fulfilling work—whether paid or unpaid, inside the home or out in the world—is essential in order to be a complete individual and equal partner.

At the same time we need to balance the needs of our marriage with the demands of our work. If we focus on volunteering or career at the expense of time with our mate, our relationship suffers. If we immerse ourselves in our marriage and let work slide, our self-esteem goes down the tubes.

Both occupation and love must be carefully cultivated so that we have a life of our own and a life together.

Affirmation: Meaningful work makes me a better mate.

CHANGE

November 3

It's astonishing in this world how things don't turn out at all the way you expect them to!
—*Agatha Christie*

As a twenty-two-year-old bride I had my entire life mapped out. The first year we'd work hard and save money, the second year we'd get pregnant, the third year we'd buy a house.

Life rarely turns out according to plan. Usually it turns out better.

Things change, we change. New career opportunities emerge, pregnancy takes longer than we'd hoped, our dream house is way over our budget.

As life changes, we need to remain open and consciously remake choices right for us today. At thirty-nine I can safely say life has turned out infinitely better than if it had unfolded as I'd planned.

Affirmation: I welcome the unexpected.

That is what learning is. You suddenly understand something you've understood all your life, but in a new way.
—Doris Lessing

At its best marriage is illuminating. Our perceptions are shaken. We're pushed to gain deeper insight into who we are and what we believe.

Life looks different as we gaze through the eyes of our mate: He gives us fresh feedback on the dynamics in our family; we expose him to the political views we fervently hold.

Each of us moves a little, thanking each other for the gift of learning, for the gift of understanding the world in a new way.

Affirmation: Thank you for opening my eyes.

"I DON'T WANT TO MOVE TO PHILADELPHIA!"

November 5

SCENE FROM A MARRIAGE: She gets a fabulous job offer that involves moving halfway across the country. You love your job. You're locked in a battle of wills. "What about my life?" she asks. "What about mine?" you counter.

This is a tough one. You need to stop fighting each other and start talking about the pros and cons of making such a big move.

Here are some factors to consider: Will taking the new job benefit both of you? How hard will it be for him to find work in a new city? Is this a long-term or short-term arrangement?

It's easier to compromise when you approach the issue as allies. If this move will tear your marriage apart, don't do it no matter how good a career opportunity it seems. If, however, one person's pride is in the way, swallow it. Remember, your commitment is to help enhance each other's life in every possible way.

Affirmation: Let's talk about it.

Suffering . . . no matter how multiplied . . . is always in-dividual.

   —Anne Morrow Lindbergh

When our partner hurts, we hurt. We anguish over his suffering and want to do everything in our power to lessen it.

We feel helpless. We wish we could come up with answers—anything to make the pain disappear.

But ultimately each of us struggles with suffering in our own way. What we can do for each other is listen, care, and help create a safe place in which our partner can release the pain. Just being nearby is sometimes the most anyone can do.

Affirmation: I would do anything to ease your pain.

RIGIDITY

To oppose something is to maintain it.
—*Ursula K. Le Guin*

Conflicts can become a tug-of-war, with each of us locked in position at opposing ends of the rope. Sometimes we hang on because we're passionate about our beliefs, willing to defend them to the bitter end. Other times our egos get in the way.

Regardless of how compatible we are, we're bound to disagree. About little things, such as whether to drink skim milk or 2%; big things, such as whether to join a synagogue or church.

Rigidly defending our position is a waste of energy. We infuse even the unimportant issues with more power —and polarity—than they warrant. Instead we can open ourselves to compromise. To hearing each other. To loosening our grip on being right in favor of finding a right place we both can be.

Affirmation: I'll give you some rope.

November 8

Treat your friends as you do your pictures, and place them in your best light.

—Jennie Jerome Churchill

Many of us are nicer to our friends than to our mates. We give them a break when they screw up. We accept their foibles, forgive their failings. We encourage and support them and stand up for them in the face of criticism.

We should be so generous with our mate. If we give our partner the benefit of the doubt, accentuating his finest qualities, downplaying his imperfections, we achieve three goals: We frame him so that others can see how wonderful he is. We reinforce him to play from his strengths. And he even looks better to us.

Affirmation: I see the best in you.

November 9

It was the best of times, it was the worst of times.
   —*from* A Tale of Two Cities, *by Charles Dickens*

Ask any couple who's celebrated their silver and golden anniversaries: They will tell you that marriage is the best of times and the worst of times.

We rejoice in the moments of triumph: our first home, the careers we nurture, the day our child takes her first step.

Likewise together we weather adversities, learning—from a lesson plan of life's obstacles—that we can truly depend on one another to navigate hard times between us.

In times of joy we turn to each other and say, "I am grateful you are here." In times of trouble we turn to each other and say:

Affirmation: I am grateful you are here.

The universal human yearning is for something permanent, enduring, without shadow of change.
—*Willa Cather*

We marry, in part, for security. To know there is one person with whom we will travel through the seasons, who will stick around for years and years, who will be a constant, fixed partner for life.

Our lives are full of upheaval; one day we're happily pruning our garden, the next we're sifting through the ashes of a fire. One day our parents are healthy, the next we're running to intensive care.

Marriage is no protection against calamity. But knowing we have a committed partner helps us pick up and start anew.

Affirmation: You can count on me.

COOPERATION

November 11

With our work schedules and lack of interest in cooking, we both knew a lot about frozen food. How could I not fall in love with her?

—Garry Trudeau (of wife, Jane Pauley)

Combining lifestyles is one of the great challenges of marriage in the nineties!

With high-pressure schedules, high-intensity jobs, and barely enough time to rest, much less whip up home-cooked meals, cooperation is the key.

Life—and marriage—today is not necessarily what we imagined it. Whatever happened to the knight on the white horse who would support you? What happened to keeping the home fires burning while he was out battling the big, bad world?

Today we are equals, which sometimes means being equally worn out and equally undernourished. We *both* must pitch in—with income, cleaning, sticking the microwave pizza in the oven—if we are to stay healthy and happily in love.

Affirmation: Let's lend a hand.

If you are afraid of loneliness, don't marry.
　　　　　—Anton Chekhov

Although Chekhov's warning sounds cynical and fore-boding—as if marriage itself increases feelings of loneli-ness—in fact he speaks of a paradox. In marriage we are both alone and together. Apart and a part of a whole.

　　Marriage in and of itself neither intensifies nor amelio-rates loneliness. We can support, encourage, and em-pathize with each other, but ultimately we are on our own. As we go through our daily lives, we realize that no matter how close we are to our mate, we are still separate individuals, each responsible for our own destiny.

Affirmation: I walk my own path, sometimes alone, sometimes with you.

GRATITUDE

November 13

How do I love thee? Let me count the ways.
  —*Elizabeth Barrett Browning*

Counting our blessings is a worthwhile daily discipline for married couples.

Each day we begin by acknowledging three ways in which we love and appreciate our mate, in which being together enhances our lives, in which we are grateful for his or her existence on this earth.

All too often our gratitude gets lost as we focus on the negatives. We take the good things for granted, concentrating on what's missing.

Anything we take for granted becomes lost to us. We recover the positives by consciously saying:

Affirmation: How do I love thee?

1. _____.
2. _____.
3. _____.

The loving are the daring.
> —*Bayard Taylor*

It takes real audacity to love another person. Many attempt it, but not all reach the summit.

Those who dare to stretch the limits of their minds and hearts to be worthy of love's ongoing tests are courageous indeed.

There are moments when we just summon the courage to climb another step. When it would be simpler to fall back, content in our solitude, protected from having to come through yet again.

Then we need to remind ourselves of all we get in return. In daring to love we become whole. In daring to love we stand on mountaintops that cannot be reached by any other route.

Affirmation: I dare.

EXPERIENCE

Love is what you've been through with somebody.
    —*James Thurber*

We enter into marriage full of anticipation. Our love is partly based on the future, on all the wonderful things we imagine will come to fruition over the years.

It is only with time that real love blossoms. Whether we're married five, fifteen, or fifty years, it is shared experience that cements our devotion. Through good times and not-so-good-times we learn who each other really is, discover our mate's character, and work together in partnership. Over time our love deepens beyond anything we could comprehend at the outset.

Anticipation is eventually overtaken by experience. We know whom we love and why.

Affirmation: Every day brings us closer.

SCENE FROM A MARRIAGE: It's your birthday. He walks in, all smiles, and hands you a huge box wrapped in newspapers and ribbons. What could it be? "Hurry," he says, "Open it!" Inside is a sleeping bag. "Surprise!" he says, "We're going backpacking for your birthday!" You hate camping. You hate carrying anything bigger than your purse. Your idea of a vacation is a hotel suite with room service. He looks at you expectantly. What now?

Do you shove the sleeping bag back in its box? Or do you pretend to be thrilled and go buy long underwear?

Neither. You have another option. You can thank him for the wonderful gift. Then you can either agree to the camping trip if you're up for an adventure or you can tell him the truth, hoping not to hurt his feelings.

Too hard-hearted? Remember, *he* chose the sleeping bag. He's the one who's dying to go camping. If you're willing to try, great! Jump in. If not, don't feel guilty or obligated. It's your birthday. You don't have to spend it lying on the ground.

Affirmation: Honesty is the best policy.

SEXINESS

I think what makes someone sexy is like what makes Beethoven's Fifth Symphony beautiful. It's the sum of a lot of things.
—*Phil Donahue*

"In Marlo's case," says Phil in a *Cosmo* article asking famous couples, "What made you fall in love with her?" "it's the way she looks, the way she communicates."

The sum total—the undefinable mix—of what draws us to our mate is different in every case. His slanted grin and the way his brow furrows when he's concentrating drives you wild with desire. Her easy laughter, slender neck, and the way she fits perfectly in your lap make you want her more than you've ever wanted anyone.

All this factors into the magic of marriage: the little things that attract us to our partner (it's an old line but she *is* beautiful when she's angry), that shine through when we're upset or disgruntled make us know, without a doubt, that we have found the right person.

Affirmation: I respond to you as I do to no one else.

A man may be said to love most truly that woman in whose company he can feel drowsy in comfort.
—George Jean Nathan

It's so sweet just to curl into each other and relax!

When I was eighteen years old, the idea of lying in bed (snuggled or not) watching the ten-o'clock news and falling asleep made my skin crawl. I would *never* be reduced to such boring domesticity.

At thirty-nine I crave the comfort and security of drifting off in the arms of the man I love. Not having to dress up. Not having to dazzle him. Just being close together as the sun rises and sets.

Affirmation: Good night, my darling.

COMMUNICATION

November 19

Women like silent men. They think they're listening.
—Marcel Achard

It's true! Often we're attracted to the "strong, silent type." We interpret his silence as attentiveness, his distance as mysterious and alluring.

Silence can be a real gift. Some men are thoughtful; they listen hard, carefully considering before offering a response.

Other men simply check out. They're remote. Or disinterested. Or don't have anything to say.

If you talk and aren't sure what's happening on the other end, ask. Don't assume he's busy flexing his ears; don't assume he's wishing you'd shut up. And don't feel embarrassed for talking too much. It's fine to be verbal. It's also fine to be quiet, as long as you find a way to communicate.

Affirmation: I can hear you.

For flavor, instant sex will never supersede the stuff you have to peel and cook.
—Quentin Crisp

Instant soup never quite tastes like the homemade broth we lovingly simmer over a slow fire.

Likewise the sex we have at the beginning of a relationship, no matter how spontaneous and fresh, doesn't begin to compare with the depth and flavor of lovemaking between long-time partners.

The time we take is worth the effort. We cultivate a more savory intimacy when we peel back the layers of who each of us really is and learn to cook to taste. It is infinitely more nourishing to know with whom we are making love.

Affirmation: Let's cook.

FRIENDSHIP

November 21

More than half your friend is lost to you when he falls in love.
—*Madame De Sartory*

Unfortunately friendship is often a casualty of marriage. We become so involved that we let our other relationships slide.

Every part of our life is diminished when we forget about our friends. Neglected, they go elsewhere for the companionship they need. Our world becomes smaller; we lose the special closeness and perspective only a friend can provide. Our marriage becomes ingrown; we suffer for lack of other input and support.

Our friends may tolerate our absence, but they won't wait around forever. It's up to us to ensure that they know, however in love we are, that we still love them as much as ever.

Affirmation: My friends still matter a lot.

"IF YOU DON'T GET OFF THAT COUCH, I'LL . . ."

SCENE FROM A MARRIAGE: He's a couch potato. He admits it. He lives on junk food, never exercises, and has a remote control growing out of his hand. You're worried about his health and you're sick of sitting around the house eating Doritos. You love to exercise. How can you get him off his butt?

You can't. But what's keeping you from working out and eating right?

Your frustration is understandable, but there's little you can do about your mate's lifestyle. You can educate him, tell him why this is important to you, ask him to make changes, but ultimately your best bet is to set a good example by being as health conscious as you can.

What you do have control over is your own choices. Here are a few things you *can* do:

1. Take charge of cooking healthier meals, or compromise—junk food twice a week, balanced meals the rest of the time.
2. Get off the couch and get going! If you need an exercise buddy, find a friend to share walking, biking, swimming, or aerobics. If *you* make a commitment to exercise, you'll stop resenting him and start feeling better about yourself.
3. Let go. Trust that he is a responsible adult who will eventually make the right choices—for himself. Until then stop criticizing and start encouraging.

Affirmation: I can't change him. I can take care of myself.

November 23

Are there any brothers who do not criticize a bit and make fun of the fiancé who is stealing a sister from them?
—*Colette*

We want our parents and siblings to embrace our mate. Their approval matters! It says, "We trust your judgment and we see what you love in each other."

Some people just click; overnight they are one big family. Sometimes it's oil and water, there is tension and animosity. We're caught in the middle. Tempers flare when we feel torn between our family and our mate.

There are lots of reasons for this: protectiveness, jealousy. Unexamined feelings of loss and abandonment keep family members from graciously extending themselves.

Give it time. Tell them how much their acceptance means. If, over time, it isn't forthcoming, don't allow them to drive a wedge between you and your mate.

Affirmation: We are each other's family.

> *i am affable*
> *i am laughable*
> *i am capable*
> *i am educable*
> —*Terry Kellogg and Marvel Harrison*

This lovely affirmation from the book *Hummingbird Words* is worth repeating daily. It helps us remember that we have everything it takes to make our marriage work.

I am affable: I am open and receptive to knowing and being with you.

I am laughable: I will nurture my sense of humor. Lighten up. Laugh at myself when I need to. Laugh at what's difficult when it will help.

I am capable: I can already do so much to show my best self in this marriage.

I am educable: What I don't know, I can learn. I am eager to grow.

Affirmation: I am all of the above and more.

FIDELITY

November 25

Faithfulness is one of the marks of genius.
 —*Charles Baudelaire*

Having an affair is easy. It doesn't take brains or talent to run away from the problems in our marriage by finding solace in another's arms.

It *does* take intelligence—and lots of it—to resolve difficult issues and continually discover how to keep our passion alive.

Ultimately everyone discovers that extramarital affairs solve nothing. They are a temporary distraction from reality that only create more problems and worse pain.

Our marriage deserves better. And we are capable of better—if we use our brains and believe in ourselves and the strength of our union.

Affirmation: I won't take the easy way out.

Our relationship is too judgmental, too demanding, too prickly to have much in common with the quiet waters of friendship. But we are each other's family.
—Anna Quindlen

Our mate needn't be our best friend, although it's nice when that happens.

Many couples are more like Scarlett and Rhett than Ozzie and Harriet; passions run high, communication takes as much concentration as learning Chinese when you grew up in Mexico.

Sometimes it seems weird that our friends understand us perfectly whereas we have to struggle for clarity with our mates. On the other hand whom do we wake up in the middle of the night when we're anxious about a deadline? Who is the first person we rush to tell when the phone rings with good news? Who is our fellow dreamer, with whom we share our deepest hopes and yearnings for all the years to come?

Family is forever, even when it isn't easy. That's a lot to count on!

Affirmation: You're my family.

CRAZINESS

November 27

The key to a successful marriage is that both partners don't get to be crazy at the same time.
— *Marlo Thomas*

Marlo Thomas made this comment in a television interview with Barbara Walters.

I agree wholeheartedly. I like the idea that we get to take turns being shaky or neurotic or just a little crazy. How nice to count on the freedom to be at loose ends once in a while, without jeopardizing our relationship.

Plus her advice is realistic. We each go through periods when we're not at our best. It helps to know that we can go through these times secure in our partner's love, confident that we won't be subject to shame or disapproval. Hopefully we are equally supportive when it's his turn.

Affirmation: It's okay when either of us doesn't have it totally together.

I tended to place my wife under a pedestal.
  —*Woody Allen*

Good old Woody Allen—always turning the well-worn cliché upside down.

Of course placing our beloved under a pedestal is no better than enshrining him or her on one. Although the original concept has some romantic appeal, in either case the old "pedestal principle" puts impossible pressure on our partner: to be perfect and flawless, to live up to—or perhaps beyond—our expectations. Plus, who can reach them when they're up so high?

Adoration is nice, but in moderation. We can admire our mate and can think the world of each other, as long as each of us has the freedom to be a real, down-to-earth human being.

Affirmation: I adore you.

INSECURITY

November 29

Anxiety is love's greatest killer. It makes others feel as you might when a drowning man holds on to you. You want to save him, but you know he will strangle you with his panic.
—*Anaïs Nin*

We're anxious about work and nudge our mate to rave about how capable we are. Our weight's up eight pounds and we wait and wait (and get mad) when he doesn't notice the new black sweater that makes us look thinner.

When we feel insecure, it's natural to want our partner's reassurance. But it doesn't help. Because our anxiety lies deep within. Nothing he can say will ease the primal feelings of insecurity that are ours alone to grapple with.

When we appoint him Ghostbuster rather than facing our demons head-on, we place undo stress on our relationship. He feels the extent of our desperation and runs away, helpless to stave off the panic. At these times we need to turn inward—not to our partner—to recover our grounding and self-esteem.

Affirmation: It's time to keep myself afloat.

Don't bother me with love, baby. Let's just go walking in the rain.

—Billie Holliday

Sometimes we talk too much. We process our relationship to death instead of living in it, relishing each other's company, walking hand-in-hand through the rain.

Cherished time spent together goes farther to cement our love than anything we could possibly say about it. Being fully in our relationship—painting the bathroom, sharing favorite old movies, quietly watching the sunset —is the best testament to our feelings. We know—deep in our hearts—that we are together. Nothing more needs to be said.

Affirmation: Be with me.

EXPECTATIONS

December 1

Limited expectations yield only limited results.
—Susan Laurson Willig

We mustn't settle, assuming our partner isn't capable of coming through for us. Neither must we saddle each other with unrealistic demands.

When we expect too little, we create a self-fulfilling prophecy; our partner lives down to our lowered expectations. "Why try?" he thinks to himself, giving up before he starts.

Ironically, overly high expectations yield the same result. Here again, we say, "Why try?" unwilling to risk failure.

It is up to each of us to develop high, but reasonable, expectations—asking for what we want with confidence in our partner's capabilities. And accepting when he or she falls short.

Affirmation: I expect everything. I accept everything.

Make yourself a blessing to someone.
—*Carmelia Elliot*

What does it mean to be a blessing to other people?

To comfort and ease their suffering. To be a reflection of their beauty. To be a stimulus for learning and growth. To be an agent of happiness and joy.

Being a blessing to our beloved means we go beyond the everyday contract of matrimony to find the sanctity in our union. Our partnership becomes a prayer: we ask for our partner's health and well-being; we give thanks for his or her presence in our life.

Affirmation: Bless you.

ANGER

December 3

Because society would rather we always wore a pretty face, women have been trained to cut off anger.
—*Nancy Friday*

Women have a tough time with anger. We've been taught to swallow our feelings, to pretend everything's fine when it's not.

We fear reprisals: If I tell him I'm angry, he'll lash back. If I broach a difficult issue, he'll blame me for causing problems in our relationship.

But unexpressed anger eventually gets its way. Often it comes out sideways: in biting sarcasm or blaming disappointment. It gets bigger, louder, and more predictable the longer we suppress it.

We need to take a deep breath and say what we feel, however frightening. If we express anger in the present, we keep it from growing into an unmanageable gulf between ourselves and our mate. Anger may not be pretty, but . . .

Affirmation: Better now than later.

SCENE FROM A MARRIAGE: You just finished third in the class on your graduate-school exams. Wow! You're thrilled and relieved and can't wait to tell him. You rush into the restaurant where you're meeting him for dinner and spill out the great news, waiting for his congratulations. But what does he say: "After all that studying, you came in third?"

There's no doubt *he* does not go to the head of the class. What's going on here?

Maybe he feels threatened. Maybe he resents how much time you've spent studying. Maybe he spent his whole life trying to get his parents to love him, despite the straight A's he brought home since he was six.

None of which makes you feel any better. It's important to understand the reasons behind his resistance to lavish praise. But it's equally important to tell him—straight out—how you feel about his reaction.

If possible, hold on to your temper. *Don't* call him names, *Do* ask for what you want. Say, "I feel great about how I did. I'd really like you to acknowledge my hard work and share my pride."

If you ask for what you want, rather than making *him* feel bad for making *you* feel bad, you might be able to start over and enjoy a happy ending.

Affirmation: I need your support, not your criticism.

UNCONDITIONAL LOVE

December 5

When you love someone, you love him as he is.
—*Charles Peguy*

If this was true, we would all have perfect marriages!

We *want* to love our mate unconditionally, fully accepting him exactly as he is. But our own needs, our ever-present ego, and our judgments get in the way. We try to change and control and correct him in the hope of transforming him into the person we want him to be.

It is a life's work to learn to love our partner without making him over in our own image. He is perfect, just as we are perfect. Perfectly able to change when and if he sees fit.

Affirmation: I love you as you are.

For many years when anyone said "I love you" to me, I would become flustered. I didn't know whether to respond by saying "Thank you," by repeating "I love you, too," or by asking "Why?"

—*Anonymous*

Sometimes we don't know what to do with the affection that comes our way. We feel overwhelmed or unworthy; we can't imagine how we could possibly be deserving of our mate's affection. We worry that since we can't put our finger on what we're doing to earn it, it may disappear as quickly as it came.

Then we want reassurance: "a list of why you love me, as detailed as possible, please."

But no such printout exists. We can try to quantify it. We can try to put it into words. But what makes him love us is greater than the sum of our acts. It is simply who we are. All we need to say is:

Affirmation: Thank you.

TRUST

December 7

No amount of therapy or analysis can heal a heart that cannot trust.

—Marion Woodman

Many of us are wounded. We go into our love relationship desperately wanting to trust, yet incapable of doing so. Our past quietly—or loudly—haunts us, making it impossible to risk vulnerability and know we will be safe.

Therapy is one step toward learning to trust. But nothing compares with practice. Each time we open our hearts, allowing our partner in far enough to test whether we can love without losing ourselves, our trust is strengthened. And when we hurt each other, as we inevitably will, we can learn—together—what it is we need to be safe. Little by little we replace old hurt with empowerment, healing, and hope.

Affirmation: Please give me time.

December 8

Where love is concerned, too much is not even enough!
—*P.A.C. de Beaumarchais*

There's no such thing as too much love. Too much dependence, yes. Too many problems, certainly. Too much suffering in relationships that aren't worthy of our energy and commitment.

But a healthy relationship never suffers from too much love or affection. The stronger the flow, the more the marriage flourishes.

If you are stingy with love, ask yourself why. Are you afraid that giving too much will make him take you for granted or mask serious issues? Are you worried you may run out?

No chance. Love replenishes itself.

Affirmation: I have an infinite supply of love.

EXPRESSION

December 9

I like not only to be loved, but to be told I am loved.
—George Eliot

Me too.

We all need it said, even when we are secure in our partner's affections.

Hearing, "I love you, you're the greatest thing that ever happened to me," is the sweetest song of all. The words themselves make us feel cherished, important, make our hearts swell.

It isn't enough to love each other. We need to shout it, sing it, whisper it in each other's ears.

Affirmation: Tell me.

Love is like a mine. There are passages, caves, whole strata. You discover entire geological eras.
—Christopher Isherwood

Within each of us lies a vast subterranean world. We dig deeper and deeper, unearthing whole new veins of our psyches, discovering nooks and crannies and passageways we didn't know existed.

Anyone who has excavated knows the process takes time and patience. We carry our lantern and proceed carefully with respect for the layers of experience that make each of us unique.

If ever we feel bored in our marriage—as if there's nothing new to learn—it's a sign to go deeper into the dark, with faith that we will discover more and more the deeper we dig.

Affirmation: There is so much more to discover about you!

JEALOUSY

December 11

As a jealous man, I suffer four times over: I suffer from being excluded, from being aggressive, from being crazy, and from being common.

—*Roland Barthes*

Jealousy isolates and alienates us. We are trapped in a prison of our own making.

Jealousy makes us angry and violent. We rush to defend what's ours for fear of losing it.

Jealousy makes us feel slightly insane and out of control. We turn into someone we neither recognize nor like.

Jealousy erodes our integrity. We lose self-respect and honor.

Jealousy is human. We are all subject to it. We are all capable of rising above it, expressing our fears, and asking for the reassurance we need.

Affirmation: My jealousy diminishes both of us.

SCENE FROM A MARRIAGE: You've talked about it, examined your finances, and agreed that it's time. To buy your first house, that is! You spend all day Sunday house shopping, only to discover a major glitch: You've fallen in love with the classic colonial, while he's sold on the sixty-year-old, beaten-down Cape Cod. "It'll be a fun project," he says, trying to persuade you. You can just picture it: weekend after weekend stripping wallpaper and sanding floors. The Cape Cod is cheaper, but it's about as far from your dream house as it gets.

You both have veto power. You can compromise on style, price range, and even location, but ultimately if one of you is opposed, it's time to keep looking.

Maybe you need to step back and discuss your visions for a home. Make a list of your priorities and compare where they match and where they diverge. Talk about your most ideal fantasies as well as what trade-offs you're willing to make.

Both of you need to be at home where you live. This is too big a decision to make hastily. If you move slowly, taking lots of time to look, you're sure to find a house you are both happy to call home.

Affirmation: Let's take our time.

MEMORIES

December 13

People forget years and remember moments.
                    —Ann Beattie

Do you remember the first time you laid eyes on him? The first kiss? The first moment you knew—in your heart—that this was the person with whom you wanted to spend the rest of your life?

The years and years fade to warm-hued background, while memorable moments emerge as touchstones of our romance. The snapshots: holding hands in front of the SOLD sign of our first house; cutting the umbilical cord after thirty hours of labor; our first Christmas, decorating the tree together.

We paste these pictures in our photo albums and carry them in our hearts. They remind us what makes it all worthwhile.

Affirmation: We have so many moments to look forward to.

A happy marriage is a long conversation which always seems too short.

—*André Maurois*

Sex is great. Going on trips together is exciting. But long talks deep into the night are one of the best ways we become really close.

Respect and curiosity are renewed each time we engage in stimulating conversation. We learn new things about ourselves and each other. Our worldviews are challenged, a broader viewpoint gained through the eyes of our beloved.

Hunger for more conversation tells us we're with the right person. Knowing there are thousands of interesting things to talk about keeps us eager for more time with our mate.

Affirmation: Can we talk?

BALANCE

December 15

On one end of the spectrum is passion; on the other safety. People tend to either have passionate but unsafe relationships or safe relationships without passion.
—*Terence Gorski*

Where there is passion without safety, we are attracted yet afraid. We feel so much, but we are never sure our connection is secure. If the flame goes out, what will be left of our love?

Where there is safety without passion, we are comfortable yet something is missing. We yearn to be ignited.

Both are terribly important. And one without the other isn't enough to sustain a long-term committed relationship.

Passion and safety aren't mutually exclusive. Our passion can flare when securely anchored; our safety allows us to be swept away by our mate.

Affirmation: I want you and I trust you.

*Marriage is not just spiritual communion and passionate em-
braces; marriage is also three meals a day, sharing the workload
and remembering to carry out the trash.*
—Dr. Joyce Brothers

How do we keep the spark alive on Tuesday nights at
seven o'clock facing a sinkful of dishes, a pile of bills, and
three loads of laundry before we can begin to think about
sex, much less sitting down in front of the TV together?

Here's a practical tip: Do it together. You'll get it done
faster, have more fun, and maybe even complain together.

Here's another one: Make a date at least twice a week
to go out for dinner, a movie, or a walk in the park.
Anything that removes you from the daily pressures and
renews passion and romance.

And, no matter what, remember that there are days,
even weeks, when you may feel more like roommates
than lovers, then suddenly you're all over each other
again. If that happens—and it will—don't be scared. This
is a good chance to get lots done around the house. Soon
the passion will return.

Affirmation: I'm willing to wait.

PRIDE

December 17

I feel like you had me ordered—and I was delivered to you—to be worn—I want you to wear me, like a watch charm or a button hole bouquet—to the world.
  —Zelda Fitzgerald, in a letter to F. Scott Fitzgerald

We want to be shown off. For our partner to wear their love for us on their sleeve.

There is a difference between possessiveness and pride. Possessiveness implies ownership; we objectify our partner and see him as a reflection of ourselves. Pride means we take pleasure in our mate, in who he is and in the fact that he has chosen us.

The first says, "I expect you to enhance my image." The second says:

Affirmation: I am honored to be with you.

The perfect mate, despite what Cosmopolitan *says, does not exist, no matter how many of those tests you take.*
—*Suzanne Britt Jordan*

1. Does your husband wake you up each morning with fresh-brewed coffee and a kiss?
2. Is your wife a tycoon in the boardroom and a tigress in bed?

This genre of questions is vaguely useful as a basis of comparison, as a means of figuring out where we are. But in reality we have to put down the magazine and look within our hearts to see how we really feel about our mate.

No one can tell us whether he's good enough or right enough; each relationship has its share of 1s and 10s on the self-help scale. There is no perfect mate, no ultimate quiz, there is only an ongoing process of learning to love another human being, in all his glory, in all his imperfections.

Affirmation: Our marriage gets an A-plus.

December 19

The best way to hold a man is in your arms.
—*Mae West*

Leave it to Mae West to shoot from the hip on the subject of love.

As usual she's right on the money. There are circumstances—more often than we realize—when holding each other tightly does more than all the loving words we could say. The safety and comfort of each other's arms, whether a gentle hug or passionate embrace, softens conflicts, reinforces closeness, and goes a long way toward cementing our commitment.

The truth is, the best way to hold a man—or a woman—is often.

Affirmation: Hold me.

Love is absolute loyalty. People fade, looks fade, but loyalty never fades.

—*Sylvester Stallone*

Absolute loyalty means standing firmly by our mate's best interests every single time. Regardless of the circumstances. Regardless of whatever else is going on in our relationship. Even when our perception of what's in his interest differs from his.

It's important not to confuse loyalty with blindness. We are required to support our mate, even when we don't agree with him. We *aren't*, however, to censor our honest opinions in order to appease him.

Loyalty in marriage simply means that our mate comes first. And when the going gets tough, the tough get loyal.

Affirmation: I won't betray you.

DREAMS

December 21

Keep true to the dreams of your youth.
          —*Friedrich von Schiller*

All her life my friend Kay wanted to play the flute. It was her husband's fortieth birthday gift to her, his way of helping to keep the dream alive.

One purpose of our union is to help us to actualize our dreams, not to put them in a drawer because finances or lifestyle or convenience take precedence.

Sometimes we let our dreaming die out as we grow up.

This is something we must be very careful of: to be flexible to change in our marriage without ever compromising our inner essence.

We must help each other recover and be true to the ideals of our youth: to write beautiful music or jump out of airplanes or whatever it is that made our heart sing at three or at twelve or at twenty.

Affirmation: Have I told you I've always wanted to _____?

When you are in love with someone, you want to be near him all the time, except when you are out buying things and charging them to him.

—*Miss Piggy*

The honeymoon almost came to an abrupt end when he threw a full-fledged tantrum in the middle of a ritzy boutique in Los Angeles, disgusted by my heart-pounding, single-minded, adrenaline-pumping, clothes-gathering pilgimage, during which I not only forgot I was married, I totally forgot he existed.

When I came to, I was shocked and disappointed at his utter lack of appropriate awe at all the possible outfits I could coordinate in fifteen minutes flat. We never went shopping together again.

It was one of the best decisions of our marriage.

Affirmation: I think I'll surprise him!

FLEXIBILITY

December 23

Love does not insist on its own way.
—I Corinthians

When I see a couple just falling in love, I'm always struck by the same thing: They attend to each other raptly and seem more interested in listening than proving their point.

Some things are worth arguing over; most aren't. Even when we don't agree, love has a way of making dissension not only possible, but a positive way to coexist. We accept our partner and let go of our need to convince him that ours is the right—or the only way—to go.

Instead we go forward together. Sometimes agreeing. Sometimes disagreeing. But always respectful and open to the other's point of view.

Affirmation: I'm listening.

SCENE FROM A MARRIAGE: He's made it perfectly clear, he couldn't care less about going to midnight Mass. In fact it's about the last thing he wants to do. It's important to you. No, it's very important to you. From the time you were a little girl, you've loved the magic of Christmas Eve. "Please," you say. "Okay," he agrees. But he doesn't want to, and you know it. "Forget it," you say, "I'll go alone. Okay?"

No. Not okay.

This one matters enough for him to make the effort graciously without making you feel bad for having asked.

In the best of all possible worlds we wouldn't have to ask. Our partners would know intuitively what matters to us. They would want to accommodate us, willingly, without arm-twisting or resentment.

But no one can read minds, and we don't always want the same things. Being willing to go out of our way for each other is enough. To say honestly, "I'll do this for *you*, because I love you and love seeing you happy."

Affirmation: Thank you.

TRANSFORMATION

December 25

Those who are married live happily ever after the wedding day if they persevere in the real adventure which is the royal task of creating a more loving world.
    —Robert Runcie, Archbishop of Canterbury

Today, on Christmas, let us remember that marriage consists of more than two individuals loving one another.

The purpose of our union goes far beyond what we give to each other. Hopefully the love we share inspires us to reach out to others and help build a more peaceful, just, and safe world.

The message of Christmas is: We renew our commitment to acts of love and healing. The message of marriage is: Together we are stronger in our ability to make a difference.

Affirmation: Together let us create a better world in which to live.

Love is an act of endless forgiveness.
—Peter Ustinov

It's easy to appreciate the ways in which our partner pleases us. It's harder to remain steadfast when we feel hurt or disappointed.

That's when we need to concentrate on loving versus worrying about how well we're being loved. That's when we need to tap the compassion deep within to forgive and go on.

It is a gift to know we can screw up and be forgiven, that we needn't fear abandonment. This is real love: no fear. Only doing our best and trusting we can love and be loved no matter what.

Affirmation: We forgive each other.

AWAKENING

December 27

I must raise myself to a higher level in order to rouse new impulses in her.

—*Vincent van Gogh*

Amazing that even van Gogh wrestled with the wish to rouse impulses in another person. Marriage challenges all of us to find new ways to rise above the mundane and discover creative ways to awaken one another, both sexually and otherwise.

We must ask ourselves this question: Am I alive? Really alive, in every pore of my being? Are my senses open? Am I doing everything in my power to stretch my awareness, develop my powers of expression, ask great things of myself so that I have more to offer?

The potential is limitless—both for our own personal growth and for what we give to one another.

Affirmation: I'm reaching for the sky.

For five whole years I see her every day, and always think I see her for the first time.

—Jean Racine

How do we keep marriage fresh? How do we retain the thrill of anticipation when our partner enters the room and walks toward us?

Experience shows it is near impossible (and perhaps medically inadvisable) to maintain a raised-heart-rate level of attraction and excitement day after day in the company of our mate. What *is* possible are moments—even days—when that shivery feeling of being in love returns. When we're struck by our partner, amazed by his beauty, her originality. When once more we can't keep our eyes off the person.

Trust in these moments. They're worth waiting for.

Affirmation: Have we met before?

SELF-CARE

December 29

Self-care isn't selfish. It's self-esteem.
—Melody Beattie

We are each fully responsible for taking good care of ourselves. Sometimes we come first, other times we put our needs on hold, always conscious of what's most vital in the moment.

The better we care for ourselves, whether it's rest, healthy food, friends, a concert, or taking a yoga class on Wednesday evenings, the more whole we are. We build more internal strength and serenity to draw upon.

Marriage consists of two healthy, well-developed individuals who respect their own well-being enough to make it a priority.

Affirmation: I have the self-respect to care for myself.

> *Grow old along with me!*
> *The best is yet to be.*
> —Robert Browning

I'm reminded of the Beatles lyric: "Will you still need me, will you still feed me, when I'm sixty-four?"

Sounds like light-years away. But as each day of our marriage passes, we become better companions, more trusted friends, and more devoted to sharing a lifetime.

How can we be sure our commitment will last? Can we count on our mate loving us into our later years?

We can trust in the timelessness of love. Beyond that, marriage is an exciting, unpredictable roller coaster in which we hold tightly to one another, hoping the ride (with fewer straight vertical drops, please!) will continue forever.

Affirmation: I can't wait!

AWE

> *And I felt so good inside*
> *and my heart felt so full,*
> *I decided I would set time aside each day*
> *to do awe-robics.*

—Lily Tomlin *in* The Search for Signs of Intelligent
Life in the Universe, *by Jane Wagner*

The end of one year. The beginning of another.

We are one year older. Hopefully we are wiser and
surer of ourselves, more aware of what it takes to make an
"affair of love" the most fulfilling adventure in life.

As we start anew, let our hearts be filled with gratitude.
Filled with appreciation for our mate. Filled with desire
for what lies ahead. Filled with the conviction that we
continue on the right road.

Let's say the special words again: "I do." We utter
them with awe and hope.

**Affirmation: Here's to another wonderful year
together.**

INDEX